Joy,

With my best wishes for a successful personal & artist life!

Best,
Rob
Oct. '07

# Baby Bird
# and Chick Carving

## Rosalyn Leach Daisey

77 Lower Valley Road, Atglen, PA 19310

**Shorebird Carving** Illustrated by Rosalyn Leach Daisey. Four projects including the Greater Yellowlegs, the Semi-Palmated Plover, the Dunlin, and a Sanderling in flight. ISBN:0-88740-219-4   Hard Cover   $49.95

**Songbird Carving**, illustrated by Sina Patricia Kurman. Five songbird projects: Black-capped Chickadee, Tufted Titmouse, American Goldfinch, House Wren, and Catbird.
ISBN: 0-88740-057-4   Hard Cover   $45.00

**Songbird Carving II**, illustrated by Sina Patricia Kurman. Five songbird projects: male and female Northern Cardinal, House Sparrow, Blue Jay, and American Robin. ISBN: 0-88740-119-8   Hard Cover   $45.00

**Upland Game Bird Carving** Illustrated by Rosalyn Leach Daisey. Five projects: male Mourning Dove in flight, perched female Mourning Dove, female Woodcock, her chicks, and a Bobwhite Quail. ISBN: 0-88740-349-2   Hard Cover   $49.95

Published by Schiffer Publishing, Ltd.
77 Lower Valley Road
Atglen, PA 19310
Please write for a free catalog.
This book may be purchased from the publisher.
Please include $2.95 postage.
Try your bookstore first.

We are interested in hearing from authors
with book ideas on related subjects.

Printed in Hong Kong
ISBN: 0-88740-590-8

# Dedication

This work is dedicated to my own babes, Jason Reynard and Jenna Brooke, who are fledging into marvelous mature beings!

# Acknowledgments

My never ending appreciation to all the students who attend the seminars I teach! All of you teach me and help me to understand how best to share what I know. I sincerely thank you all!

I wish to thank Judy Schmidt for sharing the woodie duckling loss with me, and on behalf of her successful releases, thank you, Judy!

My thanks to Gene Hess of the Delaware Museum of Natural History for his helpful assistance. Thank you, Gene!

My warmest thanks to Bill Veasey for his continued encouragement and friendship! Thank you, Bill, for all you are for me and for the art form of bird carving!

My very best thanks to my buddy, Jack Holt, who is continually sharing his bird and technical knowledge with me. Thank you, Jack!

My most sincere appreciation to Ellen J. (Sue) Taylor and Douglas Congdon-Martin of Schiffer Publishing for their expertise, talents, and patience with me! By the time Sue and Doug are involved in the book process, I am burnt toast! They both lead me through the last steps toward completion with such ease and work their magic until the book becomes what you hold in your hands! Thank you, Sue and Doug, so much!

When things don't flow or go at all, and Murphy's Law prevails, Jason and Jenna are always there with encouraging words, jokes, smiles, gifts, and most importantly their presence! There are not enough of the right words to express my deep respect, admiration, and love for these two young adults. The world is a better place already with Jason and Jenna doing their magic, and they have just begun the journey! Happy trails, kids, and thank you!

# Contents

# Introduction

Baby birds are some of the cutest creatures on this earth! What is there not to like about a baby bird? Some might say that a naked baby bird just born is plain ugly. It is so ugly that it's cute! I have spent a lot of time helping to take care of all kinds of baby birds through volunteering at a local rehabilitation facility, Tri-State Bird Rescue and Research Center. The marvelous work that is done by this organization, and others like it, is to be highly applauded! They care for orphaned and injured birds, releasing them back into the wild a great percentage of the time. Since I don't do much traveling with the bird carving business in the summertime, the people at the Center have sent baby

birds home with me for short periods that have needed particularly frequent care. Often, my living room has been monopolized by a large playpen in which there have been baby chickadees, titmice, barn swallow, quail, etc. During these times, it is difficult to get much "work" done for observing the antics of the young ones hopping from branch to branch or scratching on the playpen's floor. But oh, what a difference these experiences have made in the accumulation of knowledge about and appreciation of the young birds!

Working at the Center has given me first hand knowledge of the young birds. When one washes the poop from 25 or 30 baby robins (so that it does not deteriorate their feathers), one learns first hand the anatomy of a bird! When one has 10 or 12 blue jays begging to be fed with their squawks and gaping mouths, one sees the birds "up close and personal."

If you want to make a real difference in this world, find such a bird or animal rehabilitation center near you, give of your time and money. You will gain multiples of whatever you give in knowledge and satisfaction!

There are two main types of baby birds. Precocial baby birds (chicks) are born with a downy covering, have their eyes open, and are soon able to walk and leave the nest if necessary. Examples of precocial birds include most waterfowl, game birds, and shorebirds. Most altricial birds are born naked and helpless with their eyes closed. Most songbirds and some water birds are altricial.

In this book, I have included a broad range of carving projects: two songbirds (with feathers growing in and eyes open), a chickadee and a bluebird; one game bird chick, a quail; one shorebird, a killdeer chick; and one waterfowl, a woodie duckling. If you do all of the projects, you will experience many new procedures from downy plumage to feathers. Because of the limited availability of buying baby bird feet castings, there are several alternatives demonstrated. There are standing and nestled down birds. And there are neat colors to paint!

The format of this book takes you through each step, one at a time. From carving the blank, to texturing the feathers and/or down, to making feet, to mounting the bird and painting the project, the photographs show you each step with explanations in the text. Five complete seminars wrapped in a neat package!

Carving baby birds and chicks is such fun! They are small, so it doesn't take long to complete a project (unless you happen to be taking a picture after each step!). Several of these "guys" can be done in the same length of time as an adult bird! Texturing down can be such fun and more free-wheeling than regimented feathers. And the babes are so cute! As I see it, the only problem may be that, if you give your carvings away or sell them, you will have a problem letting go of the chick. But, hey, you can always do another, or even a flock or covey! So, let's have some fun and get started!

Rosalyn Leach Daisey
Newark, Delaware

# Chapter 1
# Baby Bird
# and
# Chick Anatomy

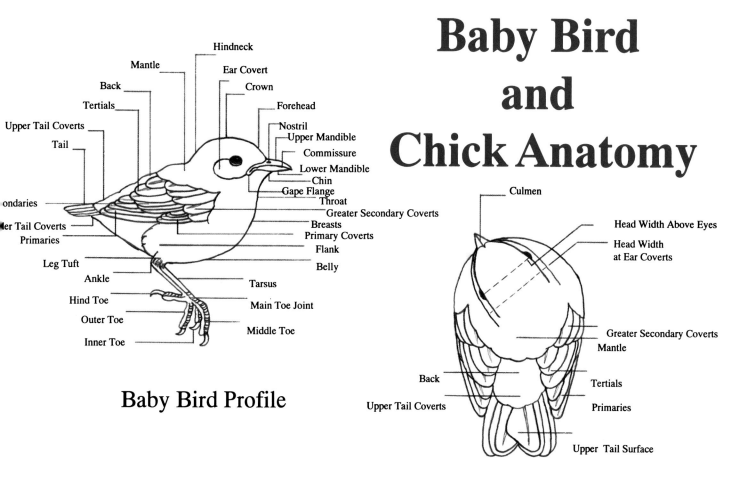

**Baby Bird Profile**

Hindneck
Mantle
Back
Tertials
Upper Tail Coverts
Tail
ondaries
er Tail Coverts
Primaries
Leg Tuft
Ankle
Hind Toe
Outer Toe
Inner Toe
Ear Covert
Crown
Forehead
Nostril
Upper Mandible
Commissure
Lower Mandible
Chin
Gape Flange
Throat
Greater Secondary Coverts
Breasts
Primary Coverts
Flank
Belly
Tarsus
Main Toe Joint
Middle Toe

**Top**

Culmen
Head Width Above Eyes
Head Width at Ear Coverts
Greater Secondary Coverts
Mantle
Back
Tertials
Upper Tail Coverts
Primaries
Upper Tail Surface

**Underside**

Breast
Belly
Vent
Lower Tail Coverts
Under Tail surface

**Chick Profile**

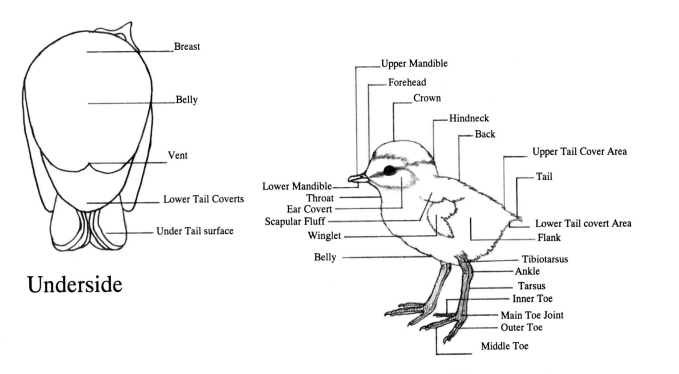

Upper Mandible
Forehead
Crown
Hindneck
Back
Upper Tail Cover Area
Tail
Lower Mandible
Throat
Ear Covert
Scapular Fluff
Winglet
Belly
Lower Tail covert Area
Flank
Tibiotarsus
Ankle
Tarsus
Inner Toe
Main Toe Joint
Outer Toe
Middle Toe

# Chapter 2
# Carolina Chickadee Baby
## *(Parus carolinensis)*

One of the most pleasing things in this life is holding a baby chickadee in your hands. I have had this magical experience quite a few times, and it is always a thrill! Every one that I have held always felt like a fluff of nothing, so small and delicate. Chickadee nests are usually located in or near deciduous woodlands. They can be found in a tree cavity or fence-post, old woodpecker holes, and bird houses. The nest cup, found 4-15 feet above the ground, is often constructed of mosses, twigs, grasses, and plant fibers with a soft lining of feathers, patches of hair or fur, or plant down. There may be 3-8 white eggs with brown spots. The female parent incubates the eggs 12-14 days. Both parents are kept busy feeding the hungry nestlings. The babies stay in the nest approximately 17 days. The parents continue feeding the young after they leave the nest until they learn to self-feed.

Baby chickadees are born naked with their eyes closed. They soon develop down for warmth and their eyes open. The feathers start becoming apparent approximately a week and a half after hatching. The feathers develop in waxy sheaths called feather tubes, which are shed when the feather grows large, pushing the tube away, and also when the bird preens itself. The inside of the mouth is yellowish with the outside gape flanges a pale yellow or white.

# Carolina Chickadee Baby

Alternate Profile Pattern
( Head up Pose )

Profile Pattern

Top Plainview of Head

Head-on View of Head

Profile View of Head

Foot

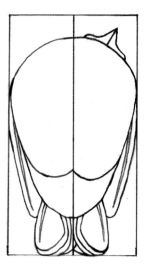

Under Plainview *

Top Plainview *

* Foreshortening may cause distortion on plainviews.
Check the dimension chart.

## DIMENSION CHART

1. End of tail to end of primaries: 0.4 inches
2. Length of wing: 1.6 inches
3. End of primaries to alula: 0.95 inches
4. End of primaries to top of 1st wing bar: 0.75 inches
5. End of primaries to bottom of 1st wing bar: 0.9 inches
6. End of primaries to mantle: 0.6 inches
7. End of primaries to end of secondaries/tertials: 0.3 inches
8. End of primaries to end of primary coverts: 0.7 inches
9. End of tail to front of wing: 2.0 inches
10. Tail length overall: 0.8 inches
11. End of tail to upper tail coverts: 0.5 inches
12. End of tail to lower tail coverts: 0.4 inches
13. End of tail to vent: 0.9 inches
14. Head width at ear coverts: 0.8 inches
15. Head width above eyes: 0.65 inches
16. End of beak to back of head: 1.05 inches
17. Beak length
    top: 0.2 inches
    center: 0.45 inches
    bottom: 0.2 inches
18. Beak height at base: 0.15 inches
19. Beak to center of eye: 0.65 inches, 4 mm brown eye
20. Beak width at base (gape flanges): 0.5 inches
21. Tarsus length: 0.6 inches
22. Toe length
    inner: 0.4 inches
    middle: 0.5 inches
    outer: 0.4 inches
    hind: 0.4 inches
23. Overall body width:1.3-1.4 inches
24. Overall body length: 2.5 inches

## TOOLS AND MATERIALS

Bandsaw (or coping saw)
Flexible shaft machine
Carbide bits
Ruby carvers and/or diamond bits
Variety of mounted stones
Pointed clay tool or dissecting needle
Compass (the kind used to draw circles)
Ruler measuring in tenths of an inch
Calipers measuring in tenths of an inch
Rheostat burning machine
Awl
400 grit sandpaper
Drill and drill bits
Laboratory bristle brush on a mandrel
Needle-nose pliers and wire cutters
Toothbrush
Safety glasses and dustmask
Super-glue and 5 minute epoxy
Oily clay (brand names Plasticene or Plastilena)
Duro ribbon epoxy putty (blue and yellow variety)
Krylon Crystal Clear 1301 Spray
Pair of brown 4 mm eyes
Tupelo or basswood block: 1.7" (H) x 1.4" (W) x 2.6" (L)
Pair of chickadee feet to use in bird or as a model
16 Gauge galvanized wire
Carbon paper

## CARVING
## THE CAROLINA CHICKADEE BABY

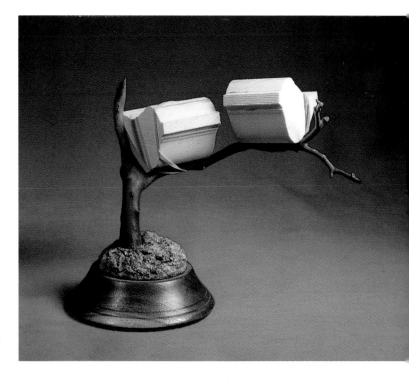

Figure 1. The mount is a piece of unsandblasted manzanita branch. Its reddish brown color will contrast nicely with the coloring of the completed baby chickadees.

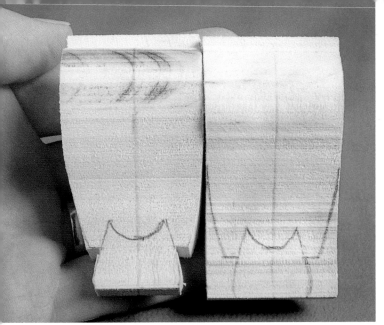

Figure 2. Transfer the profile pattern to the tupelo or basswood block and cut it out with a bandsaw. I used tupelo for these two chickies. Draw the centerline on the top and underside of the blank. It does not need to completely go down the forehead and around the end of the beak, since the head of the bird is going to be turned in the wood and not sawed off. Transfer the wings and tail part of the planview pattern. With a ruler, check that the distance from the end of the tail to the tip of the primaries is 0.4 inches and that the distance from the end of the tail to the upper tail coverts is 0.5 inches. Bandsaw or cut away the excess.

Figure 3. With a pointed ruby carver, cut around the upper tail coverts and inside edges of the primaries. Cut away the outer top edges of the tail, leaving a convex shape.

Figure 4. Redraw the tail centerline and check for balance. On the sides and tip of the tail, draw a line 0.1 inches from the top edge. The wood between the top edge and the line will be the actual tail. The wood below the line is excess and will be removed shortly.

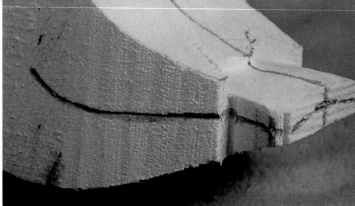

Figure 5. Using the profile pattern as a guide, draw in the lower wing edge on both sides of the blank. Note that the forward portion of the wing edge has a slight curvature, but that the rear part is straight. Check from the tail end view that both wing edges are approximately the same height. If you wanted one of the wings higher and one lower, it would be at this point in the carving process that you would draw it that way.

Figure 6. With a square-edged carbide cutter, relieve under the lower wing edge, cutting away the entire side of the flank to the corner of the blank. This is not a v-shaped cut with the corner of the cutter. The bit is laid on its side so that you will be taking the same amount of wood all the way down to the corner of the blank.

Figure 7. The cut needs to start into the wood gradually at the front, getting deeper under the wing edge as it proceeds back towards the wing tip. The depth of the cut is approximately 0.1 inches at its deepest point. Be careful that you do not dig into the side of the tail.

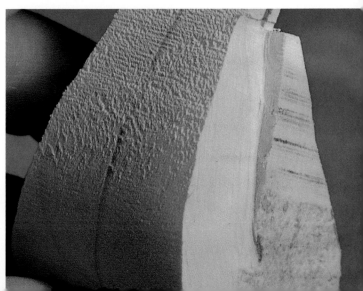

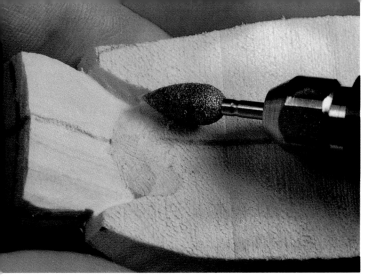

Figure 8. Round over and flow the upper tail coverts down to the base of the tail with a ruby carver.

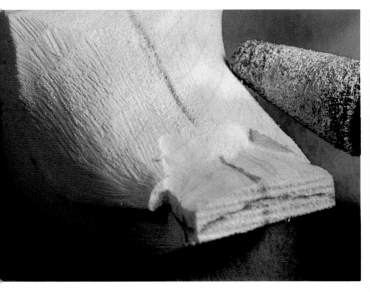

Figure 9. With a carbide cutter, round over the wings and back from the centerline to the lower wing edge on both sides. Begin the rounding cuts at the base of the neck and proceed to the wing tips.

Figure 10. On the underside, measure, mark, and draw in the lower tail coverts and vent. The lower tail coverts are 0.4 inches from the end of the tail, and the vent 0.9 inches, also from the end of the tail.

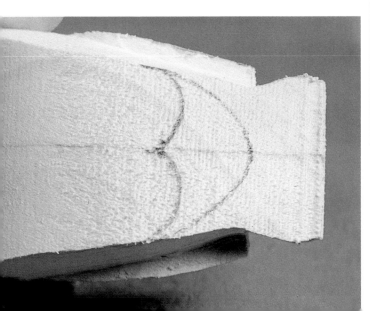

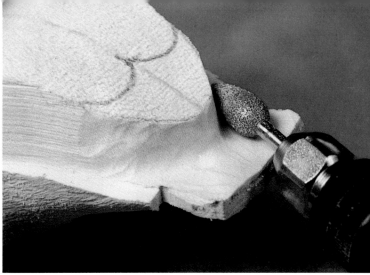

Figure 11. Use a medium pointed ruby carver to cut away the excess wood around the lower tail coverts and under the tail, leaving it 0.1 inches thick throughout.

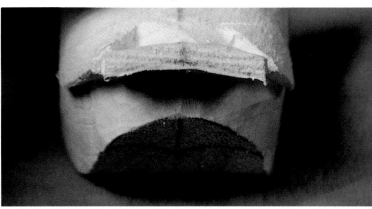

Figure 12. The concave shape of the tail's underside should correspond to the convex shape of its topside.

Figure 13. Use a small tapered carbide cutter to channel along the vent line. The channel will need to be deeper at the corners of the blank in order that the lower tail coverts can be sufficiently rounded. Failure to make it deep enough on the outer edges will make the top of the lower tail coverts flat.

**Carolina Chickadee Baby 13**

Figure 14. The channel on the side of the vent (flank) should angle toward the head and not straight up towards the back. Be careful not to nick the lower wing edges with the tip of the bit.

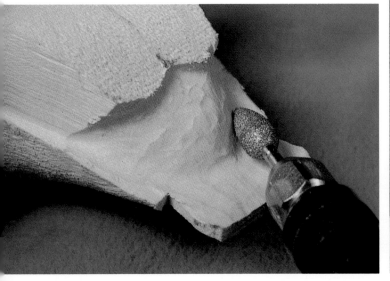

Figure 15. Round over the lower tail coverts and flow them down to the base of the tail.

Figure 16. Create a shallow channel on the centerline from the vent and up the belly 0.7 inches. Round over the belly from side to side and flow the sharp edges of the midline channel down to its deepest point. Flow the flanks and the vent area down to the lower tail coverts, eliminating the shelf created around the vent.

**14  Carolina Chickadee Baby**

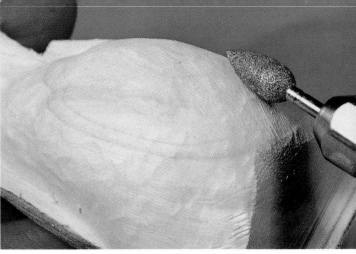

Figure 17. You do not need to round the breast yet, just the belly.

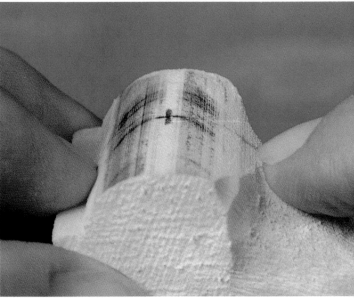

Figure 18. Find the center of the head by placing one finger at the base of the beak and another at the back of the head and sighting the middle high point. Mark the midpoint on the centerline.

Figure 19. Using this center mark as a pivot point, swing an arc from the base of the beak to the side to which you want the bird's head to turn. Do not press the point of the compass too deeply into the top of the head, especially if using tupelo which is very soft.

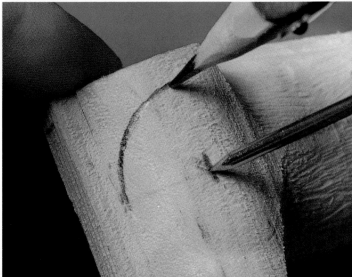

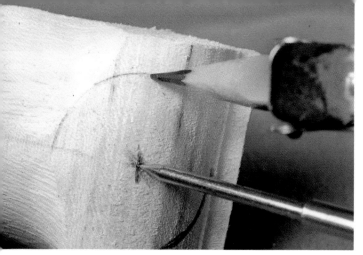

Figure 20. Without changing the dimension of the compass, swing an arc on the opposite side for the back of the head distance.

Figure 21. Changing the dimension to that of the distance from the pivot point to the end of the beak, swing another arc to the same side to which the head is to turn.

Figure 22. Draw a new head centerline through all three arcs and the pivot point. The distance between the new and old centerlines determines the amount of the head turn: the further the distance, the greater the head turn. It is helpful to erase the old centerline.

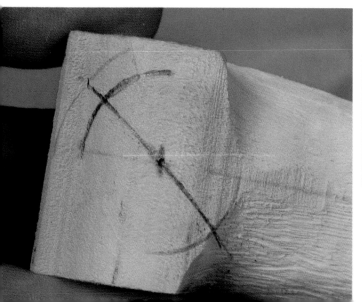

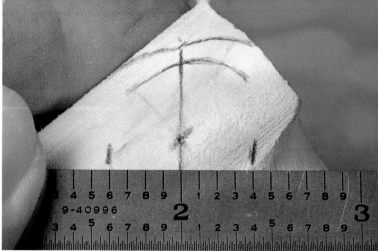

Figure 23. The widest part of the bird's head is the distance between the ear coverts. Holding a ruler perpendicular to the new centerline, measure and mark the head width at the ear covert dimension (0.8 inches)--0.4 inches on each side of the centerline.

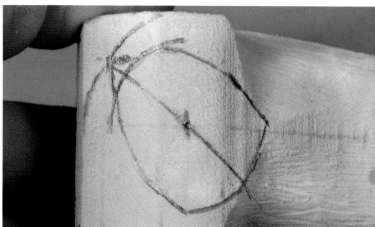

Figure 24. Draw in the top planview of the head and beak going through the measurement marks. Just draw the beak freehand without using any dimensions but allowing plenty of extra wood. The sides of the head should be straight back from the ear covert measurement marks to the back of the head arc.

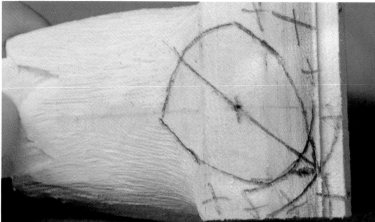

Figure 25. The wood outside of the planview drawing is the excess to be cut away.

**Carolina Chickadee Baby 15**

Figure 26. On the sides of the head draw a line along the neck area so that you do not cut into the shoulders.

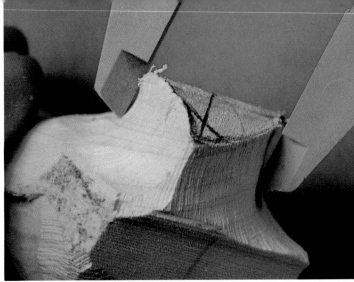

Figure 29. When the excess is removed, check to see that the dimension is 0.8 inches from side to side.

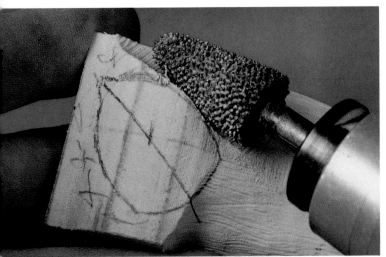

Figure 27. Using a medium tapered carbide cutter, begin cutting away the excess wood from the head and beak. Keep the sides of the head and beak straight up and down. Since the bit is round, there is the tendency to scoop out too much in the middle of the cut--DON'T! Do not cut any wood from the back of the head yet.

Figure 30. Round down the shelf on the shoulder on the side of the head turn.

Figure 28. Holding the bird low so that you can look straight down the cuts will help keep the sides vertical. You may need a smaller bit to snug up close to the line around the beak. Keep equal amounts of wood on both sides of the centerline on the head and beak to keep both balanced.

Figure 31. On the other shoulder, you can take off a little wood rounding the shoulder toward the throat.

**16  Carolina Chickadee Baby**

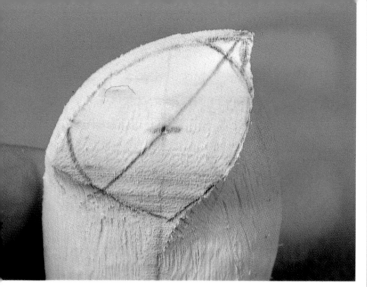

Figure 32. Remove a little of the wood behind the head. Round the shoulders and side of the breast towards the centerline on the throat and breast.

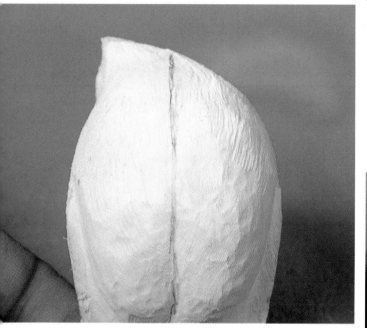

Figure 33. Keep the sides of the breast equal and round all the way to the centerline. There is a tendency not to round this area enough and thus leaving the bird square breasted and boxy.

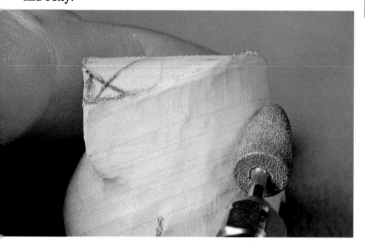

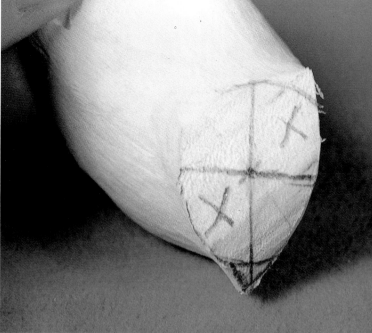

Figure 35. Turning the head of the bird in the wood causes the planes on the top of the head and, sometimes the top of the beak, to be "whoppy-john" (this is a highly technical Southern term meaning screwed up). To correct the messed up angled plane, draw a line perpendicular to the centerline on the top of the head pivot point, dividing the head into quadrants. The high side on the forehead is on the side to which the head is turned and on the opposite side on the back of the head and neck. Marking the high quadrants with "x's" helps to remind you of the high points.

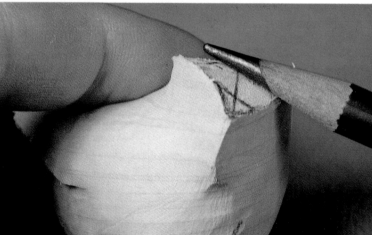

Figure 36. Holding the bird in a natural, balanced position, note the low forehead on the bird's left and the higher plane on its right.

Figure 34. Using a smooth cutting ruby carver, remove the deep scratches from the coarse carbide cutter. It is difficult to draw fine lines on a rough surface.

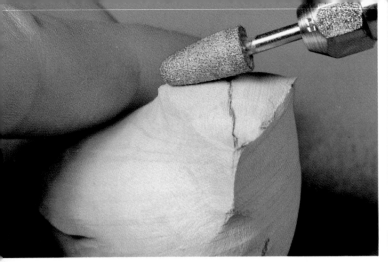

Figure 37. Level the forehead by cutting away the high side. A small amount of wood will need to be removed from the top base of the beak. In turning the head in the blank, the more the head is turned, the more wood you will have to remove to level up the head. If you have to cut away the centerline in order to achieve balance, redraw it.

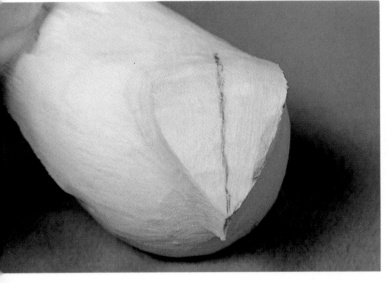

Figure 38. Holding the bird in a natural position, remove the excess wood from the back of the head and neck to level that area. Flow the hindneck down onto the shoulder area.

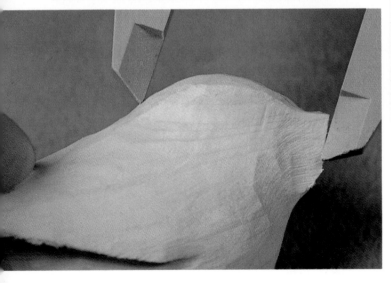

Figure 40. Transfer the eye and beak placement and shapes from the profile line drawing. Keep both sides balanced with one another. Check all the dimensions with a ruler and adjust as needed.

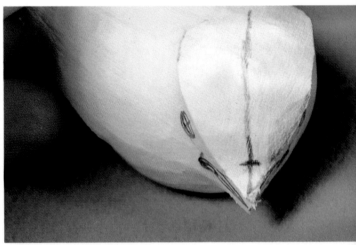

Figure 41. On the top centerline, measure and mark 0.2 inches from the end of the beak.

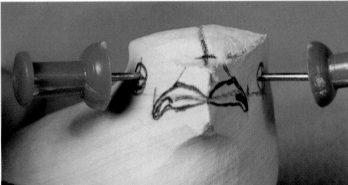

Figure 42. Using pushpins in the eye centers helps to check on the balance of the eye placement.

Figure 39. The distance from the end of the beak to the back of the head (a point halfway down the back of the neck) should be 1.05 inches. If it is too long, remove equal amounts of wood from the end of the beak and the back of the neck.

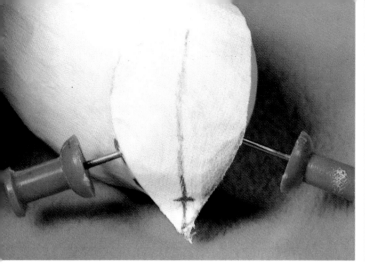

Figure 43. Also check the top planview for balance. Different shapes on each side of the head can alter the perception of balance.

Figure 46. Carefully cut around the gape flanges on both sides and underneath.

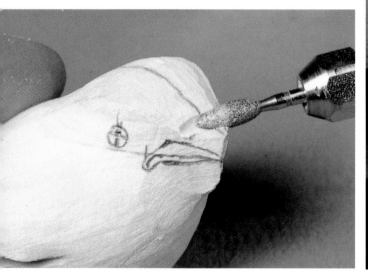

Figure 44. Using a small medium pointed ruby carver, cut straight across at the 0.2 inches mark, and remove the excess wood from above the beak.

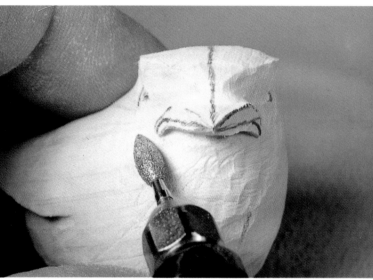

Figure 47. Check from the front end view to make sure that the gape flanges are balanced. Flow the channel that was cut around the beak and blend into the surrounding area.

Figure 45. Keep the top of the beak flat at this time. Redraw the centerline on the top of the beak.

Figure 48. Cut back underneath the beak, keeping the bottom of the lower mandible flat, until it measures 0.2 inches. Flow the chin onto the throat area, making a smooth transition.

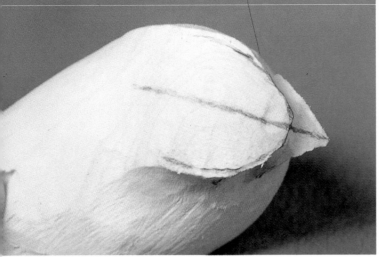

Figure 49. Measure and mark 0.65 inches across the crown above the eyes. Pinprick the eyes deeply so that the eye center positions are retained even when wood is cut away

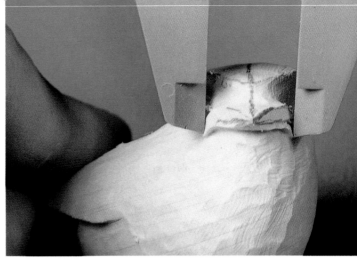

Figure 52. The width of the gape flanges should measure 0.5 inches. Adjust if necessary by removing any excess wood, making sure that the beak is balanced across the centerline. If needed, remove additional wood from around the flanges so that they project from the side of the head.

Figure 50. Narrow the head from the eye positions up to the top of the corner of the head, keeping the sides vertical. Check from the front view that there are equal amounts of wood on both sides of the centerline. Do not round the head yet.

Figure 53. Draw in the top planview of the beak. The width across the beak just in front of the flanges should be 0.18 inches.

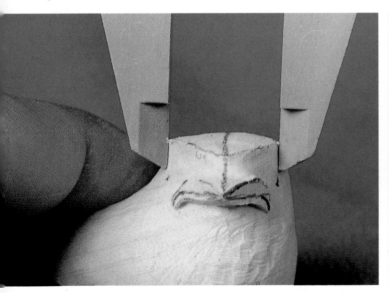

Figure 51. Use the calipers to make sure the distance above the eyes measures 0.65 inches.

Figure 54. Cut away the excess wood from the beak, keeping the sides vertical and balanced.

**20  Carolina Chickadee Baby**

Figure 55. Redraw the commissure line and check the balance of the beak and commissure line from the front end view. Adjust if necessary.

Figure 56. Angle the upper mandible from the centerline to the commissure line. There is more of an angle on the pointed part of the beak back to the flanges with less angle on them.

Figure 57. Use a stone to generally smooth the beak and lightly round over the ridge on the upper mandible (culmen) and the corners on the bottom of the lower mandible. Recheck all beak measurements and adjust if necessary. Lightly sand the beak with 400 grit paper.

Figure 58. Redraw the commissure line and recheck for balance. Lightly burn in the line holding the burning pen vertically to the side of the beak.

Figure 59. Lay the burning pen on its side and lightly burn up to the first burn line from the flanges to the tip. This two-stroke burn creates the illusion that the lower mandible fits up and underneath the lower edge of the upper mandible.

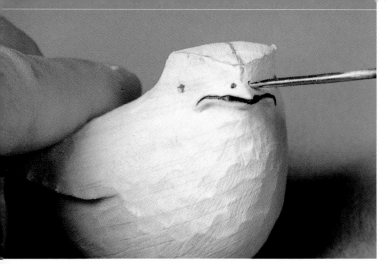

Figure 60. Mark the nostril holes, making sure that they are even. Use a sharp dissecting needle to press in the nostrils at an angle.

Figure 61. Lightly sand the beak again with 400 grit paper and saturate with super-glue. When the glue is dry, lightly sand again. The super-glue will harden any "nubbies" or irregularities on the beak's surface with the extra-fine sandpaper whisking them away.

Figure 62. Recheck eye placements for balance and drill 4 mm eye holes. Use the 4 mm eyes to make sure the holes are sufficiently deep and wide enough.

Figure 63. Round the corners of the head on the forehead, crown and hindneck. Flow the back of the head and neck down onto the mantle and shoulder areas.

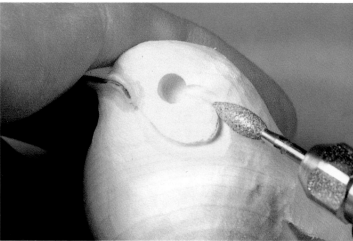

Figure 64. Draw in the ear coverts and check all views for balance. Using a small medium ruby carver, cut around the ear covert lines. Only use the point near the gape flanges and back corner of the eyes. Using the point along the entire covert will cause many, sometimes serious, digs in the wood as the point will be sucked into any soft areas. Laying the bit down and using the widest diameter will allow a much smoother cut.

Figure 65. Flow the ear covert channel out onto the surrounding area. Round over the sharp edge of the channel, giving a fullness to the covert fluff. You may need to remove a small amount of wood under and in front of the eyes. Each eye sits in a small depression.

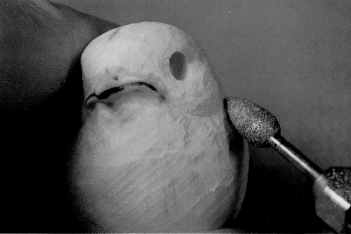

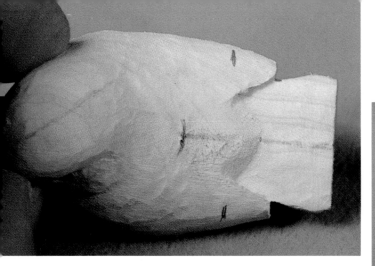

Figure 66. Measure and mark the mantle and secondary groups.

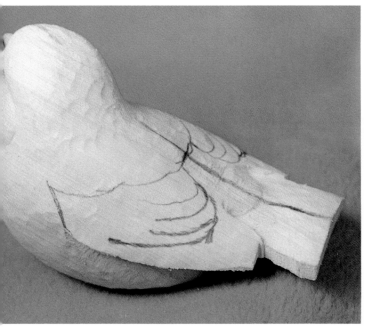

Figure 67. Draw in the mantle, tertials, lower secondary edges and side breast fluff (that covers the front portion of each wing).

Figure 68. Keep both sides of the bird balanced.

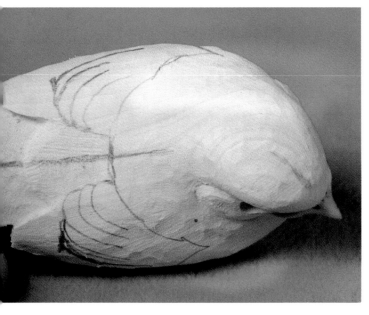

Figure 69. Laying a medium ruby on its side, cut along the mantle and side breast fluff lines. You will need to use the point to relieve the junction on each shoulder where the two lines meet.

Figure 70. Since the wings and back feathers come out from underneath the mantle and side breast feathers, flow the channel out onto the wings and back. Create a smooth transition in lowering these areas.

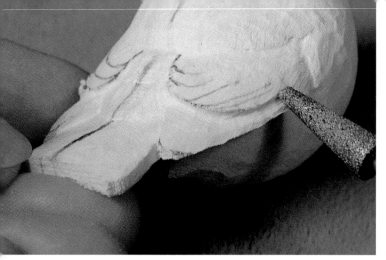

Figure 71. Round over the sharp edge of the channel on the mantle and side breast fluffs. Cut around the inside part of the tertials, their tip and the lower secondary edge on each side, leaving a sharp-edged shelf. Flow the cut out onto the primaries on each side. Round the tips of the primaries.

Figure 72. Draw in the inner edges of the primaries and remove a little wood from the back, allowing the primaries to be slightly raised. Round the edges of the tertials and secondaries.

Figure 73. You will need to remove a small amount of wood on the corners of the upper tail coverts so that they can be rounded down to the base of the tail along its outer edges.

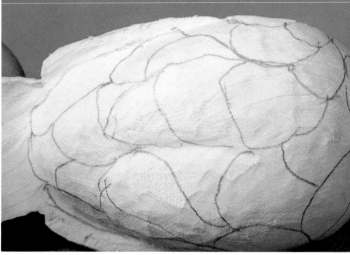

Figure 74. Draw in the random contouring lines of the feather fluffs on the underside.

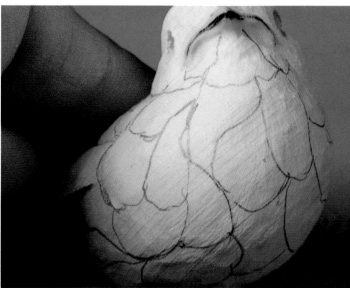

Figure 75. Keep the shapes and sizes varied so there are interesting areas to see.

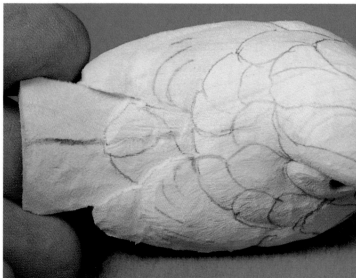

Figure 76. Also draw the contouring lines on the hindneck, mantle, and upper tail coverts.

Figure 77. Channel along the lines and round over each feather fluff.

Figure 80. With a small pointed ruby carver, carefully relieve the wood from under each lower wing edge, so that you create the illusion of the body going up and underneath each wing.

Figure 78. Using a single light source at a low angle shooting across the surface allows the contours to be seen more easily.

Figure 79. The channels on the topside of the bird should be more shallow than those on the underside. Shallower channels ensure that the contours are not as exaggerated as deeper ones.

Figure 81. Use a blunt-pointed stone to generally smooth the entire bird except for the beak. You will need to use smaller stones in some areas, such as under the lower wing edges.

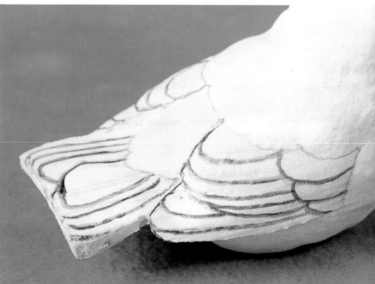

Figure 82. Draw in the feathers on the wings and upper tail.

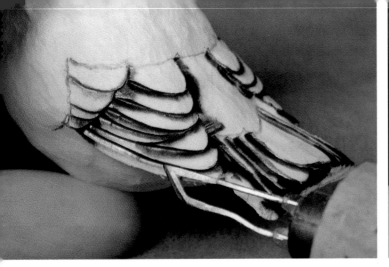

Figure 83. Lay the burning pen down on its side and burn around each feather, starting at the front of the wings and working towards the back and tail.

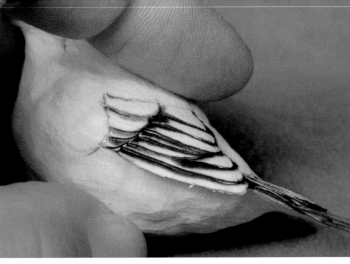

Figure 86. Hold the burning pen perpendicular to the tail's side edges and burn a line down its thickness. This will create the effect of two feather edges, one stacked upon the other.

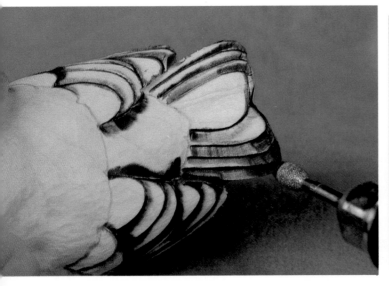

Figure 84. Grind away the excess from around the tips of the tail feathers.

Figure 87. Burn around the corner of each tail feather tip. This will indicate the inside edges on the underside.

Figure 85. Holding the ruby carver at an angle, thin just the side and end edges of the tail, leaving the center thicker for support. Lightly sand the tail's underside.

Figure 88. Draw in the trailing edges of the tail feathers on the underside. Lay the burning pen on its side and burn around each feather.

**26  Carolina Chickadee Baby**

Figure 89. Drawing in the feather shapes keeps them from becoming too large or too small. After you have done a few of these babies, you may no longer need to draw them in. Do not create a regular pattern such as fish-scales.

Figure 92. Stoning is cleaned up using the laboratory bristle brush on a mandrel. Running it at too high speed or pressing too hard will whisk away the stoning. Use a light touch and low speed and proceed with the grain.

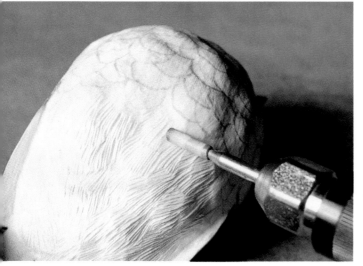

Figure 90. Using a small cylindrical stone, begin creating the barbs of each feather starting at the tip of the lower tail coverts and working up the body. Curving each stroke creates a naturalistic flow.

Figure 91. Proceed with the stoning up the belly, breast, throat and chin. Keep the stoning strokes as close as possible so that there are no unstoned areas.

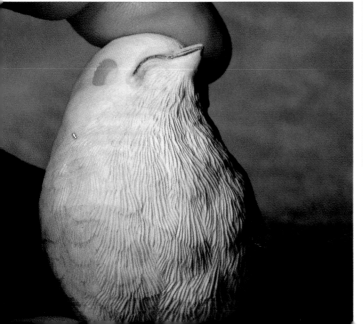

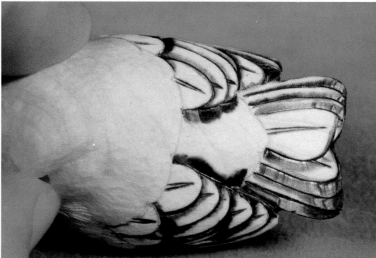

Figure 93. Draw and burn in the quills.

Figure 94. Begin burning in the barbs at the lower wing edge and proceed upward and forward, burning in the feather underneath and then the one on top. Burn the barbs on both wings.

Figure 95. Cleaning the burned areas with a toothbrush will eliminate any carbon deposits.

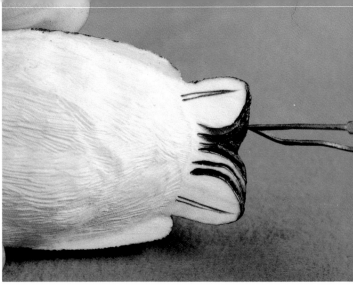

Figure 98. Draw and burn in the quills on the underside. Begin burning in the barbs on the center feathers and proceed towards the outer ones.

Figure 96. Begin burning the tail barbs on the outer feathers and work towards the center.

Figure 99. Draw and burn in the quills on the underside of the primaries.

Figure 97. Burning in a few random splits will create a realistic appearance. To burn a split, just hold the burning pen a little while longer on a particular barb, making it slightly deeper than the surrounding ones.

Figure 100. Burn in the barbs on the underside of the primaries.

**28  Carolina Chickadee Baby**

Figure 101. Draw in the feathers on the topside.

Figure 102. Note the feather pattern around the eye and on the ear covert.

Figure 103. The small bristly feathers around the eye radiate around its circumference and then flare out from the front corner towards the base of the gape flange and beak. Use the tip of the burning pen and light stabbing strokes.

Figure 104. At the front of the ear covert just below the eye, the feathers make their turn to go back to the rear of the group. The small feathers on the side of the forehead turn back toward the rear of the head on the ridge where the head was rounded.

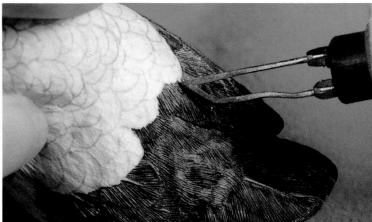

Figure 105. Begin burning or stoning the feathers on the topside at the tip of the upper tail coverts. Work up towards the head.

Figure 106. Starting at the edges of the mantle, burn up towards the neck and head.

**Carolina Chickadee Baby 29**

Figure 107. Blend the burning into the stoning along the shoulders and side breast fluffs.

Figure 108. Finish burning the barbs on the head.

Figure 109. Burn in the barbs up close to the beak where the stoning could not reach.

Figure 110. Check the eyes to make sure that the hole is sufficiently wide and deep. Fill the eye holes with clay and press into place, so that they are not too shallow or deep. Continue setting the eyes according to the directions at Figure 104 in Chapter Three (Baby Bluebird) page 67.

Figure 111. Holding the bird in a natural position, mark the position of exit points of the tarsi. The bird should be balanced over its toes.

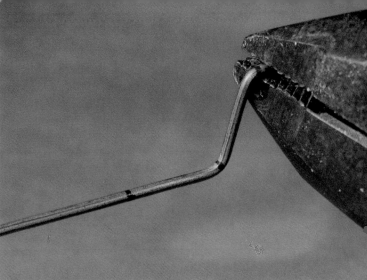

Figure 112. There is not a measurement for the exit points for the tarsi since each mount will require different placements. Generally, the placements will be forward of the vent.

Figure 115. Remove the wire from the body. Make the appropriate bends in the wire, keeping it straight between bends.

Figure 113. Using a 1/16" drill bit, drill approximately 1/2" deep holes at the marked positions. Drilling at an angle toward the head allows me to keep the correct anatomy of the tibiotarsus (lower leg) and the tarsus (actually the foot bone) in mind.

Figure 114. Insert a piece of 1/16" galvanized wire. Mark the ankle joint position right up next to the body, allow 0.6 inches for the tarsus length, and leave approximately 0.6 inches to go into the driftwood mount. I use a permanent marker to mark these dimensions so that they cannot be rubbed off too easily.

Figure 116. After the other foot is completed, hold the bird over the mount and mark the position of each foot. Spreading the feet slightly will give a more stable look to the baby.

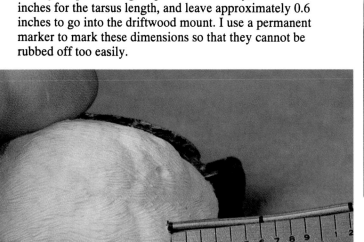

Figure 117. Using an awl to mark and start the hole for the drill bit will keep it from drifting and running wherever it wants to go.

**Carolina Chickadee Baby 31**

Figure 118. Supporting the branch so that it does not break, drill 5/64" diameter holes at the placements. Drilling slightly larger diameter holes than the wires allows you to slip them in and out of the mount more easily. On a thin branch mount, drill completely through it. You may have to adjust the bends of the foot wires until a balanced and natural position is accomplished. The underside holes can be patched and painted to blend after the bird is painted, the wires shortened, and the bird glued into place.

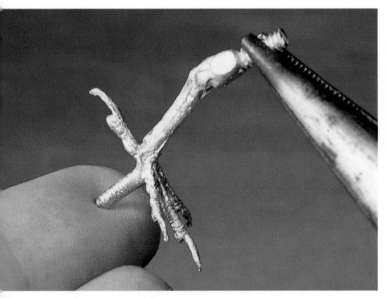

Figure 119. If desired, entire foot castings can be used instead of wire. I prefer the wire for the tarsus which allows more natural and varied positions.

Figure 120. To obtain a set of toes if you cannot make it to one of my classes, cut the tarsus and stub off above and below the toes.

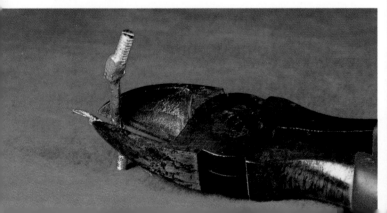

Figure 121. Mark the center of the main toe joint and start the hole with an awl to keep the drill bit from drifting. Carefully drill 1/16" diameter holes through the joint. Check the length of all the toes. Some chickadee toes are longer than necessary. Shorten the length, if needed, and reshape the claw. Do not use a ruby carver or diamond bit to cut away any excess, since the bits will become useless for cutting once they fill up with the casting material (a variation of solder). Instead, use a fluted carbide cutter. Cut away any excess casting material from the sides of the toes.

Figure 122. Note that the hind toe comes off the right side of the hole (tarsus placement) of the left toes and the left side of the right toes.

Figure 123. Fit the sets of toes on their respective wire.

Figure 124. Recheck the bird's position from all angles to make sure its balanced.

Figure 125. Normally I do not bend the toes until the bird is completely painted and ready to glue into place. With this particularly thin and delicate branch, I did bend the toes to a droop. They could not be completely wrapped around the branch, since it is advantageous to have the bird off the mount for painting.

Figure 126. Remove one tarsus and apply super-glue down into the hole. Quickly put the wire back into the body and place on the mount. Check for the proper position. Allow a minute or so for the glue to harden and do the same procedure for the other foot wire.

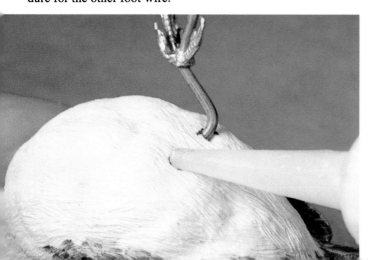

Figure 127. Place the toes on the foot wires and place the bird on the mount. Using gap-filling super-glue or 5 minute epoxy, drop just a little glue at the main toe joint. Do not put so much glue that it runs down between the casting and the wire, gluing it to the mount at this point.

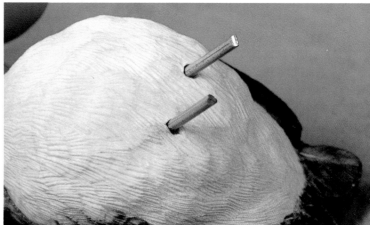

Figure 128. For the bird to be nestled down on the branch, drill one-half inch deep holes into the belly and insert pieces of 16 gauge galvanized wire into the holes, leaving one-half inch protruding.

Figure 129. Drill 5/64" diameter holes into the branch at the appropriate insertion points.

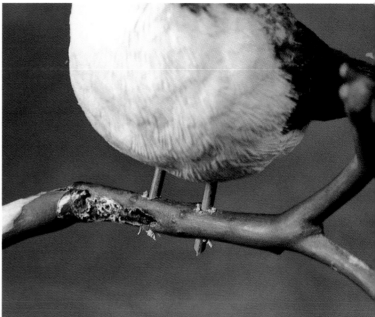

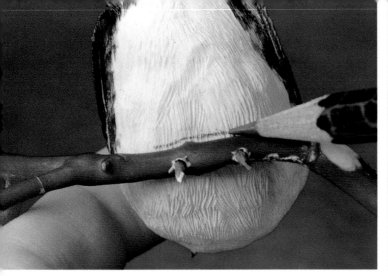

Figure 130. Mark the belly around the branch.

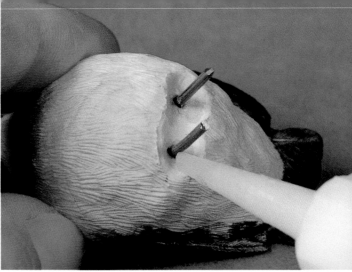

Figure 133. Glue the wires into the body.

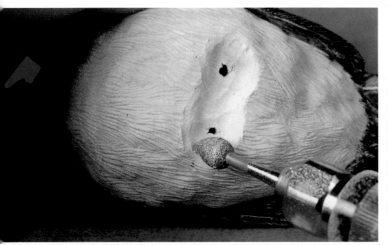

Figure 131. Relieve the area that was marked. Keep fitting the bird on the branch and removing the excess wood from the belly until the baby nestles down on the branch as desired.

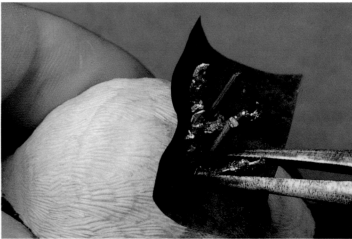

Figure 134. When the glue has hardened, slip a piece of carbon paper on the wires with the carbon side towards the body, and push each set of toes on the wires and in towards the body.

Figure 132. Prepare the sets of toes as before. Bend the toes downward as they will fit over the branch.

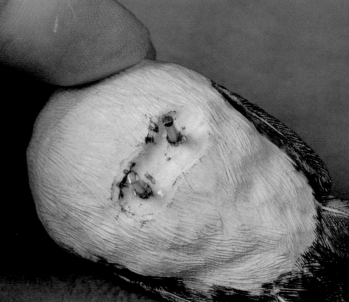

Figure 135. The carbon will be deposited on the belly at each high point of the toes.

Figure 136. Relieve all areas where the carbon marked. Fit the toes over the wires and check for fit.

Figure 137. You will likely need to use the carbon and relieve the belly several times until the toes recede into the belly feathers.

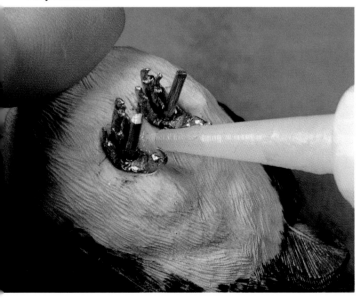

Figure 138. Fit the sets of toes on the wires and glue into place.

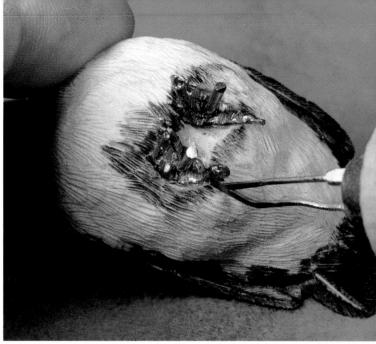

Figure 139. Burn the feather barbs around the relieved area.

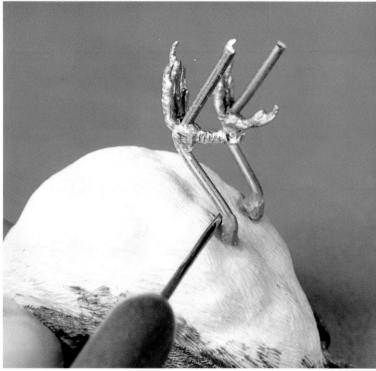

Figure 140. On the upright baby, apply the kneaded ribbon epoxy putty around the tarsi insertion points. If the epoxy putty starts sticking to the tool, press the end into the oily clay.

Figure 141. Pull the putty into the surrounding texturing to blend. Put angled texturing lines into the leg tufts to simulate hair-like feathers.

Figure 142. Apply a small amount of putty to the main toe joint and press in horizontal lines to simulate the wrinkling that occurs.

Figure 143. Spray both birds with Krylon Crystal Clear Spray 1301 and allow to dry. Using a stiff bristle brush, apply the gesso right out of the jar. Do not add water to the gesso, as the water causes tiny pinholes to develop in the surface. Load the brush with gesso, wipe most of it on a paper towel, and use a dry-brush technique scrubbing it down into the texturing grooves. The stiff bristles will keep the gesso from pooling in the bottom of the grooves and filling them up. Gesso the entire bird, feet, head, and beak included. It usually takes about two coats to even out the color differential of the stoning and burning. Sometimes, it requires a third application to cover the green putty areas. When the gesso is dry, carefully scrape the eyes.

## Carolina Chickadee Baby

Liquitex Acrylics (jar) colors:
White = W
Black = B
Burnt umber = BU
Raw umber = RU
Raw sienna = RS
Payne's grey = PG
Cerulean blue = CB
Yellow oxide = YO
Gesso
Matte and Gloss Mediums

* Indicates that a small amount should be added.

# PAINTING THE CAROLINA CHICKADEE BABY

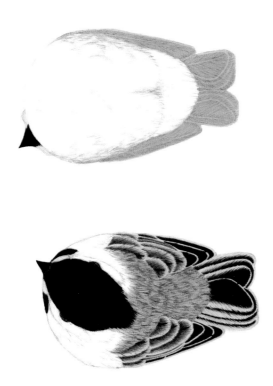

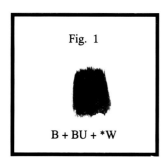

Fig. 1

B + BU + *W

Figure 1. Mixing black, burnt umber, and a small amount of white, apply several thin coats to the cap, eye ring, bib, and the beak, beginning at the forward portion of the gape flanges and out to the tip. Apply sufficient coats to cover the gesso in these areas.

Figure 2. Keeping the edges irregular will make blending the adjacent colors easier.

Figure 3. With straight black and a fine liner brush, paint in small semi-circular lines, creating a small feather pattern on the cap and bib. The feathers get slightly larger as they progress back on the head and hindneck.

Figure 4. When the feather edges are dry, apply a very thin payne's grey wash over the cap and bib. The darker feather edges should be very subtle.

Fig. 4

PG
Wash

Fig. 5

RU + CB + W

Figure 5. For the basecoats on the mantle, back, rump, wings, and tail, blend raw umber, cerulean blue, and white to a medium grey. Apply several thin coats until the gesso is covered. Be sure to cover the lower wing edges and the sides and end of the tail. Pull the mantle color into the bottom edges of the cap. To get a soft transition, pull the dark cap color into the lighter one. Working the light and dark back and forth several times will create a natural transition.

Figure 6. Adding more white to the basecoat mix, use a round sable brush flared to lighten the edges of the feathers on the mantle, back, and rump. Feather edges can be created more realistically by holding the flared brush at a right angle to the bird's surface, touching the wood, dragging the tips of the bristles a short distance, and then pulling off.

Figure 8. Do the light feather edges several times, washing in between applications with the raw umber and cerulean blue washes.

Figure 7. Blend raw umber and cerulean blue, and add a lot of water to make a thin wash. Apply the wash to the mantle, back, rump, wings and tail. Apply a super-thin raw sienna wash to these areas.

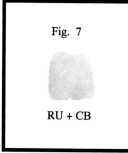

Fig. 7

RU + CB

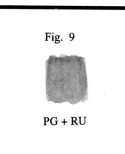

Fig. 9

PG + RU

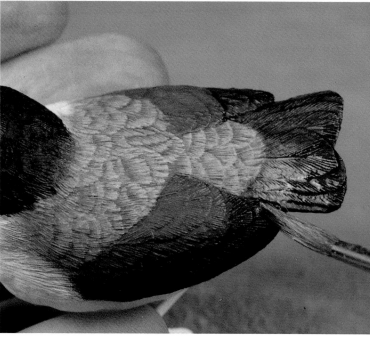

Figure 9. Apply several thin washes with a mixture of payne's grey and raw umber to the wings and tail, drying in between applications. Then, apply several more of the dark washes to the primaries and tail, so they are darker than the upper part of the wing.

Figure 10. Mix white, raw umber, and cerulean blue to a light grey, and apply wide feather edgings to the greater secondary coverts and tertials.

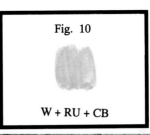

Fig. 10

W + RU + CB

Figure 12. Widen the feather edgings at the base of the tail feathers with the light grey mix.

Figure 11. Using a fine liner brush and the light grey mixture thinned with water, pull fine line edgings on the remaining wing and tail feathers. If the paint consistency is too thick, the brush will leave blobs instead of a fine line.

Figure 13. Apply a thin payne's grey and raw umber wash to the wings and tail.

**40  Carolina Chickadee Baby**

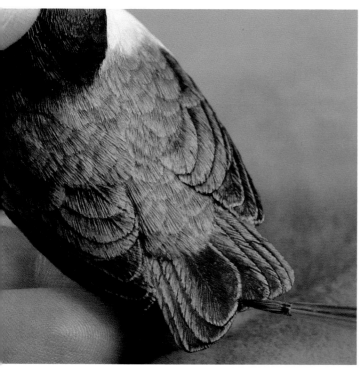

Figure 14. Alternate the light edgings and the dark washes several times until the feathers look soft. Use a mixture of payne's grey and raw umber to paint in a few random splits, to correct any squiggles caused by slipping off the edge when doing the fine line edgings, and to darken the quills on the wings and tail.

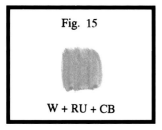

Fig. 15

W + RU + CB

Figure 15. For the basecoats on the lower tail coverts, belly, breast, and ear coverts, blend white, raw umber, and cerulean blue to a light medium grey. Apply several thin coats.

Figure 16. Blend the underside basecoat mixture into the bib's edges.

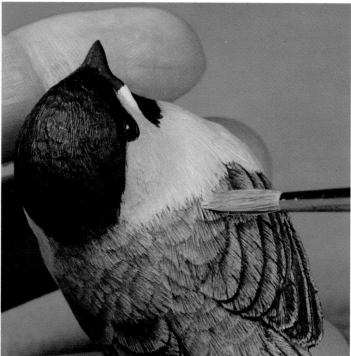

Figure 17. Lightly dry-brush the basecoat mixture over the shoulder areas blending the lighter color into the darker mantle color.

**Carolina Chickadee Baby 41**

Figure 18. Blend raw sienna with small amounts of burnt umber and white. Apply the mixture lightly to the chick's flanks.

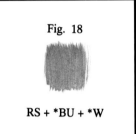

Fig. 18

RS + *BU + *W

Figure 19. Edge the feathers on the lower tail coverts, flanks, belly, breast, and ear coverts with straight white. Hold a flared brush at a right angle to the surface, touch, drag, and pull off. A smaller brush is useful to do the smaller feather edges on the ear coverts and shoulders.

Figure 20. First, apply a thin straight white wash to all of the edged areas, then add a small amount of raw umber to the white wash, and apply again.

Figure 21. For the basecoats on the underside of the tail and the underside of the wings, blend payne's grey, raw umber, and white to a medium grey. Apply several thin coats until the gesso is covered. Be careful that the thin paint does not track around the texturing edges to the topside.

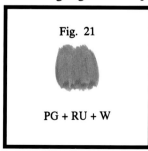

Fig. 21

PG + RU + W

Figure 22. Blend more white into the mixture, and edge the feathers. Make a wash with the edging mixture, and apply to the underwings and the underside of the tail.

Figure 24. Pull the light and dark colors back and forth several times on the side edges of the cap.

Figure 23. With a mixture of black and burnt umber, pull the bib edges out onto the lighter breast. Use a liner brush to pull fine lines irregularly spaced. Blending white with small amounts of raw umber and cerulean blue, pull the light color back into the darker one. Working the light color into the dark, and the dark color into the light creates a soft transition area.

Fig. 23

B + BU

Figure 25. Using the light detail color (W+*RU+*CB) and a fine liner brush, pull fine lines from the front of the eye to the sides of the forehead.

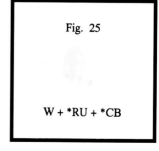

Fig. 25

W + *RU + *CB

**Carolina Chickadee Baby  43**

Figure 26. For the basecoats on the feet, blend black, burnt umber, and a small amount of white to a charcoal color. Apply several coats to the tarsis and toes.

Fig. 26

B + BU + *W

Fig. 28

W + *YO

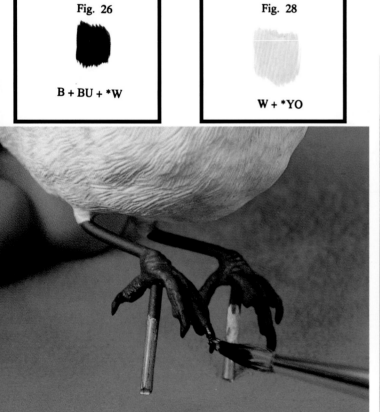

Figure 27. Apply straight black to the claws. When the claws are dry, make a wash with the black and apply to the entire feet.

Figure 28. Touch up any smudges of dark paint on the gape flanges with gesso. Blending white and yellow oxide, paint the gape flanges and a line slightly above and below the commissure line all the way to the beak's tip. It will take several coats of the yellowish-white mixture to cover the dark color out on the beak. When these are dry, apply a very thin raw umber and yellow oxide mixture wash to the entire beak.

Figure 29. Put a small amount of gloss medium into a large puddle of water, and apply to the tarsis and toes. When this is dry, apply straight gloss to each claw.

**44  Carolina Chickadee Baby**

Figure 30. Mix equal amounts of matte and gloss mediums, and apply to the beak.

Figure 31. Apply straight gloss to the quills on the wings and tail.

Figure 32. Carefully scrape the eyes. Shorten the foot wires, if needed, and glue the birds in place.

# Chapter 3

# Eastern Bluebird Baby
## *(Sialia sialis)*

Eastern bluebirds inhabit woodlands, open country, fields, parks, and gardens. The bluebird's nest can be found in a birdhouse or cavity in a tree or post usually 3-20 feet above ground. The nest cup is often constructed of dry grasses, weeds, and fine twigs, with its lining of finer grasses, hair, fur, and fine feathers.

The female bluebird usually lays 4 or 5 pale blue eggs. Sometimes Poppa will incubate the eggs, but mostly that is Momma's responsibility. The incubation lasts from 13 to 16 days. Both parents care for the young nestlings. The babies are born naked with their eyes closed. Soon they begin to develop down and their eyes open about the fifth day. The inside of their mouth is deep yellow with the outer gape flanges a pale yellow. The young leave the nest approximately 15-18 days after hatching. Poppa continues to care for the young fledglings while Momma often establishes a new nest for the next brood.

## DIMENSION CHART

1. End of tail to end of primaries: 0.55 inches
2. Length of wing: 1.8 inches
3. End of primaries to alula: 1.2 inches
4. End of primaries to top of 1st wing bar: 0.9 inches
5. End of primaries to bottom of 1st wing bar: 1.2 inches
6. End of primaries to mantle: 0.9 inches
7. End of primaries to end of secondaries: 0.5 inches
8. End of primaries to end of primary coverts: 0.8 inches
9. End of tail to front of wing: 3.35 inches
10. Tail length overall: 1.5 inches
11. End of tail to upper tail coverts: 0.5 inches
12. End of tail to lower tail coverts: 0.45 inches
13. End of tail to vent: 1.3 inches
14. Head width at ear coverts: 0.9 inches
15. Head width above eyes: 0.65 inches
16. End of beak to back of head: 1.35 inches
17. Beak length
    top: 0.4 inches
    center: 0.65 inches
    bottom: 0.22 inches
18. Beak height at base: 0.2 inches
19. Beak to center of eye: 0.85 inches, 6 mm brown eyes
20. Beak width at base: 0.5 inches
21. Tarsus length: 0.71 inches
22. Toe length
    inner: 0.5 inches
    middle: 0.7 inches
    outer: 0.5 inches
    hind: 0.5 inches
23. Overall body width: 1.6 inches
24. Overall body length: 3.35 inches

## TOOLS AND MATERIALS

Bandsaw (or coping saw)
Flexible shaft machine
Carbide bits
Ruby carvers and/or diamond bits
Variety of mounted stones
Pointed clay tool or dissecting needle
Compass (the kind used to draw circles)
Ruler measuring in tenths of an inch
Calipers measuring in tenths of an inch
Rheostat burning machine
Awl
400 Grit sandpaper
Drill and drill bits
Laboratory bristle brush on a mandrel
Needle-nose pliers and wire cutters
Toothbrush
Safety glasses and dustmask
Super-glue and 5 minute epoxy
Oily clay (brand names Plasticene or Plastilena)
Duro ribbon epoxy putty (blue and yellow variety)
Krylon Crystal Clear 1301 Spray
Pair of brown 6 mm eyes
Tupelo or basswood block: 2.0" (H) x 1.6" (W) x 3.35" (L)
Pair of bluebird feet to use in bird or as a model
16 Gauge galvanized wire

# Eastern Bluebird Baby

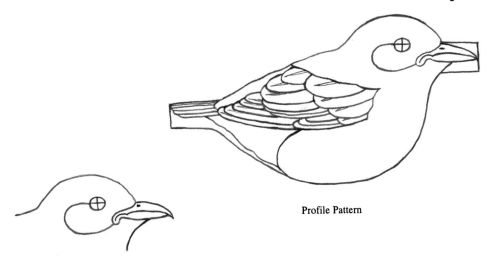

Profile Pattern

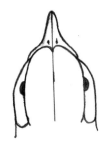

Top Plainview of Head

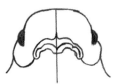

Profile View of Head

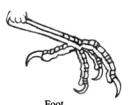

Foot

Head-on View

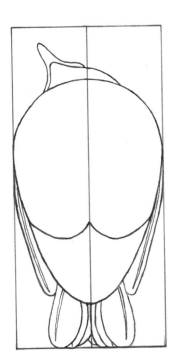

Under Plainview *

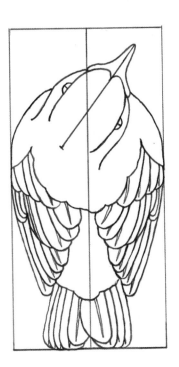

Top Plainview *

\* Foreshortening may cause distortions on plainviews.
Check the dimension chart.

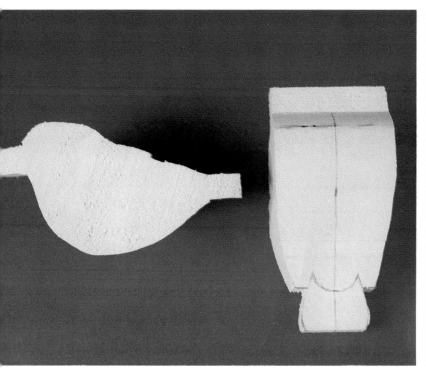

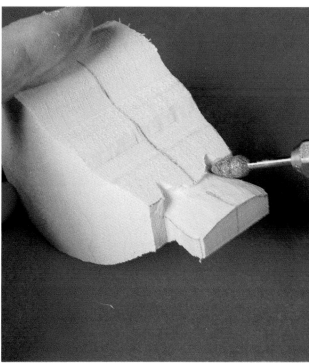

Figure 1. Transfer the profile pattern to the block of tupelo or basswood. Cut the baby out of the block with a bandsaw or coping saw. Draw the centerlines around the bird except for the beak. Using the top planview pattern as reference, transfer or draw in the wings, upper tail coverts, and tail. Use the ruler and planview drawings or the dimension chart to make sure that the drawing on the blank is correct. Bandsaw or cut away the excess from around the tail and wings.

Figure 3. With a medium pointed ruby carver, cut around the edge of the upper tail coverts, and cut away the excess wood on the top of tail down to the marked sides and end. The top of tail should be slightly convex.

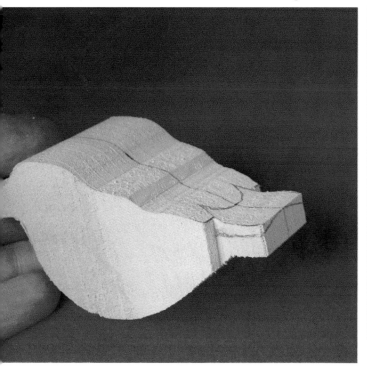

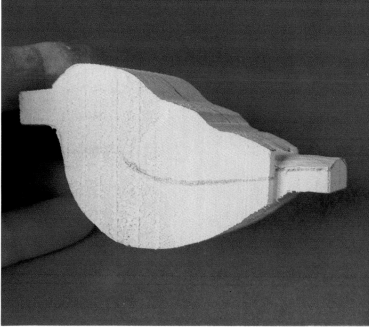

Figure 2. Draw a curved line on the end of the tail and continue the lines up each side.

Figure 4. Referring to the profile pattern, draw in the lower wing edges, making sure that they are balanced on both sides. Note that the forward part of the line is curved and then straightens as it approaches the tips of the wings.

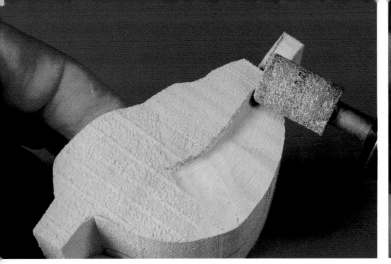

Figure 5. Using a square-edged carbide cutter, relieve the wood under the lower wing edges. Lay the cutter on its side so that the amount of wood removal is consistent on the entire flank. The depth of the cut is a gradual transition near the front of the wing and gets deeper as it progresses towards the tail.

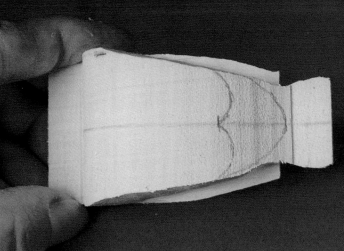

Figure 8. On the underside centerline, measure and mark the vent 1.3 inches from the end of the tail and the edge of the lower tail coverts 0.45 inches also from the end of the tail. Draw in the vent and lower tail covert shapes.

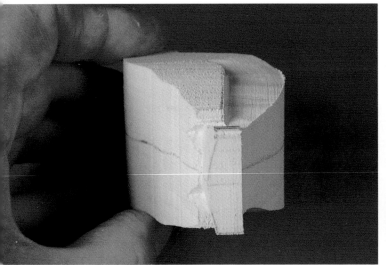

Figure 6. Note that there is equal wood removal throughout the entire flank down to the corner of the blank at the belly.

Figure 7. Beginning at the base of the neck, round the mantle, wings, and back areas from the centerline down to the lower wing edge.

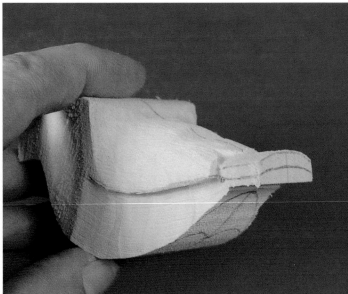

Figure 9. On the sides and end of the tail, draw a line 0.1 inches from the top edge. The wood between the top edge and the line is the actual tail. The wood below is excess.

Figure 10. Cut around the lower tail coverts and remove the excess wood under the tail. The underside of the tail should be concave to correspond to the convex plane of the top.

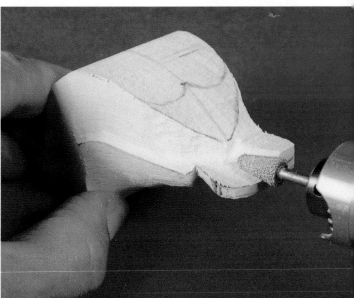

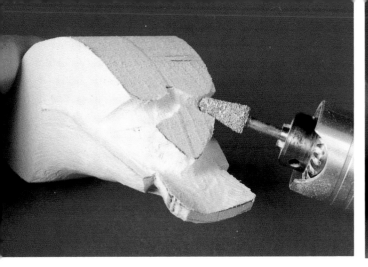

Figure 11. Using a small tapered carbide cutter, cut a channel around the vent, deeper on the corners.

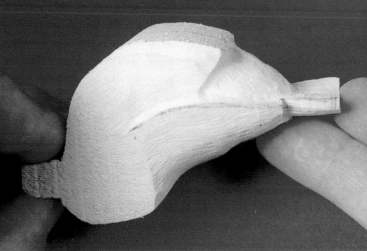

Figure 14. Flow the tail coverts down to the base of tail, eliminating the shelf created from cutting around their edges.

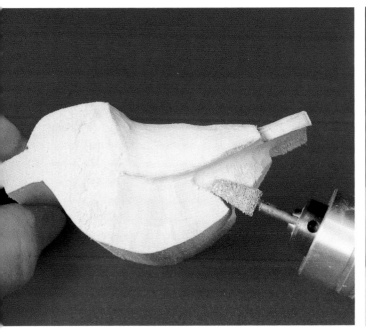

Figure 12. Cut a channel on each flank that angles toward the head.

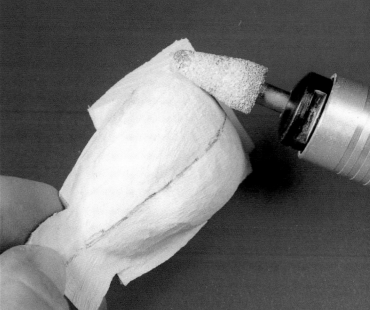

Figure 15. Cut in a shallow channel from the vent one-half inch up the belly on the centerline. Round over the belly. Flow the shelf on the end of each flank down to the side of the lower tail coverts. At the vent, round the belly down to the bottom of the shallow channel.

Figure 16. Find the center point of the head by placing one finger at the base of the beak and another finger at the back of the head (halfway down the neck). Optically choose the midpoint and mark.

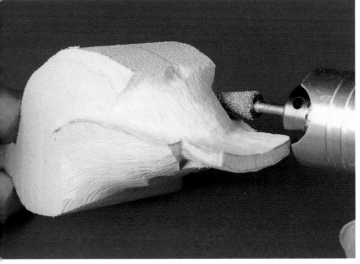

Figure 13. Round over the lower tail coverts.

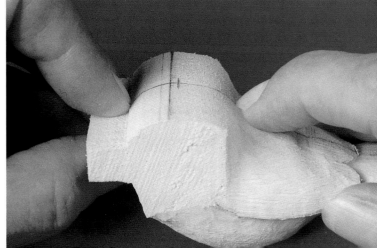

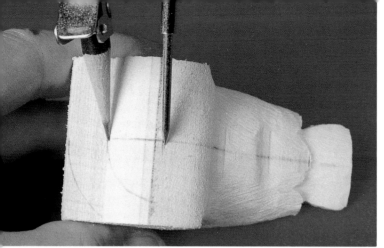

Figure 17. Place the point of the compass on the midpoint and set the distance to the tip of the beak. Swing an arc to the side to which you want the head to turn. Shorten the dimension of the compass to the distance between the pivot point and the base of the beak. Swing that dimension's arc to the same side as the head turn.

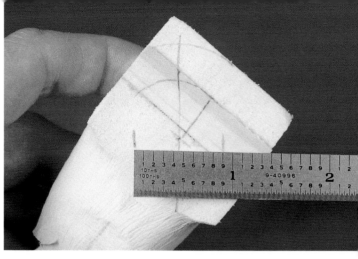

Figure 20. The widest part of any bird's head is the width at the ear coverts--0.9 inches for the baby bluebird. Hold the ruler perpendicular to the new centerline. Measure and mark 0.9 inches (0.45 inches on each side).

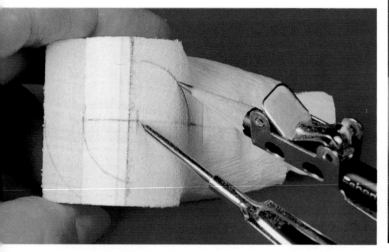

Figure 18. Using the same dimension as the pivot point to the base of the beak, swing another arc on the opposite side on the back of the head.

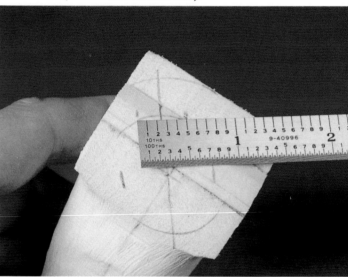

Figure 21. At the base of the beak arc, measure and mark 0.5 inches (0.25 inches on each side of the centerline).

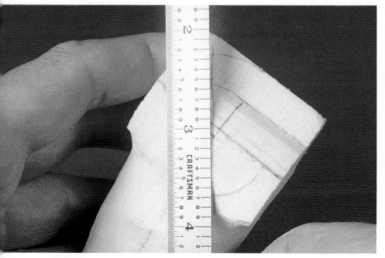

Figure 19. With a ruler, draw a new centerline for the head that intersects all three arcs and passes through the pivot point. The distance between the new and old centerlines determines the amount of head turn.

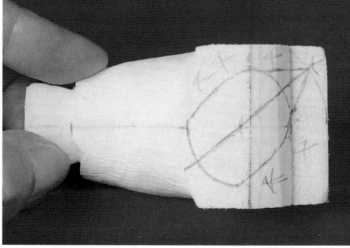

Figure 22. Looking straight down on the head, draw in the planview encompassing the measurements for the base of the beak and the width of the head at the ear coverts. All of the wood around the lines is excess.

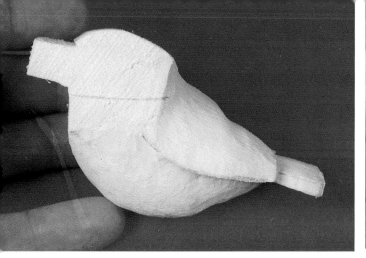

Figure 23. On the sides of the head, draw a line from underneath the beak to the back of the head.

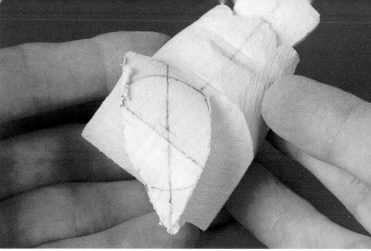

Figure 26. Looking down on the planview of the head helps in keeping the sides vertical when cutting.

Figure 24. Keeping the sides of the head and beak straight up and down, cut away the excess wood. Keep equal amounts of wood on each side of the centerline. Do not cut away any wood from the back of the head.

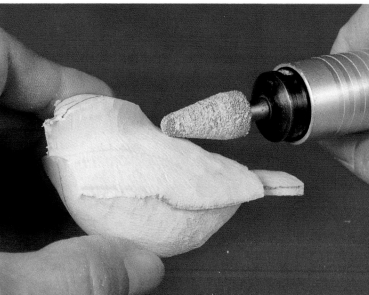

Figure 27. Flow the head out onto the shoulder and eliminating the shelf on the head turn side.

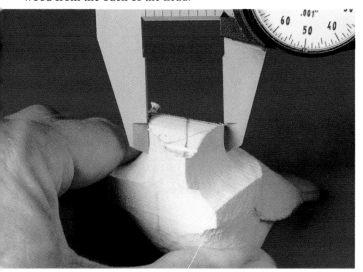

Figure 25. Use the calipers to check the head width at the ear coverts.

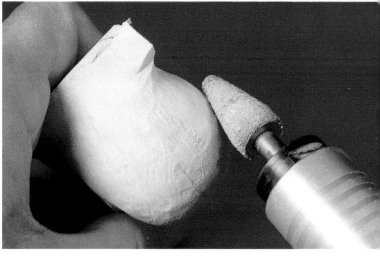

Figure 28. Round the breast from the sides to the centerline. This seems to be a problem area for many carvers. If sufficient wood is not removed on the breast, the bird looks too boxy and square-chested.

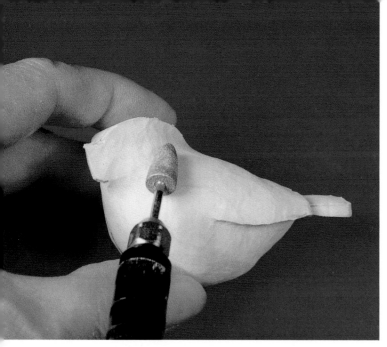

Figure 29. With a smooth cutting ruby carver, grind away the scratches made by the carbide cutter. It is difficult to draw in accurate shapes on rough wood.

Figure 30. Cutting out a bird blank from the profile view and turning its head in the wood causes the planes on the top of the head to be too high in spots. On the top of the head, draw a line through the pivot point and at a right angle to the centerline dividing the head into quadrants. On the forehead the quadrant on the same side as the head turn is the high area and the opposite quadrant on the back of the head and neck is high.

Figure 33. Cut away the high part on the back of the head and neck. Flow the hindneck down onto the mantle and shoulder areas.

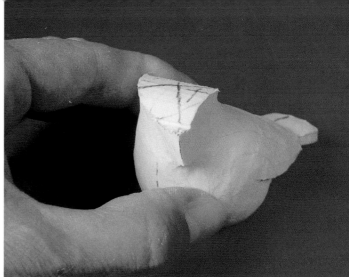

Figure 31. Holding the bird in a natural position allows you to see the goofy planes on the top of the head.

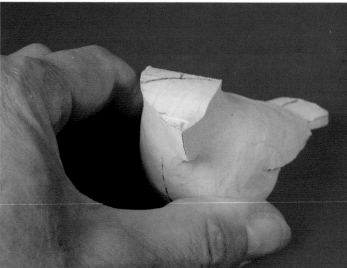

Figure 32. On the forehead, trim the high quadrant down so it matches the other side. More wood will have to be taken off the outer portion than near the centerline. Some wood will need to be taken off the high side of the beak as well. The further the head is turned, the more wood will need to be removed. Do not round anything yet.

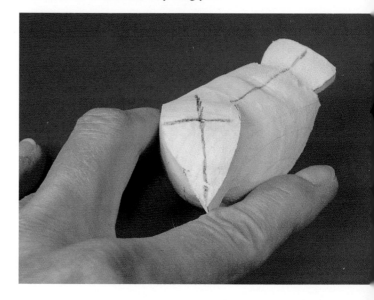

Figure 34. Transfer the beak and eye placements from the profile line drawing to the carving. Make sure the placements are equal as you look at the head from the front view. Check all dimensions with the ruler or calipers. Deeply mark the eye centers and lightly pinprick the base of the gape flanges.

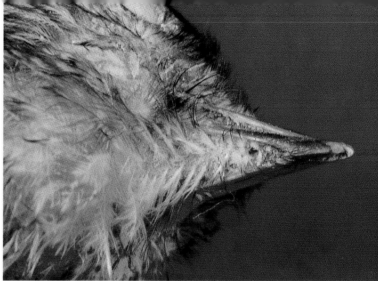

Figure 37. On the underside view of the beak, you can see the small tuft of feathers that the beak wraps around.

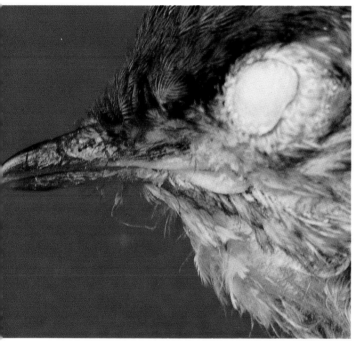

Figure 35. Note the shape of the profile view of the baby bluebird study skin.

Figure 36. On the top planview of the study skin, the beak recedes back into the feathers to form a modified v-shape.

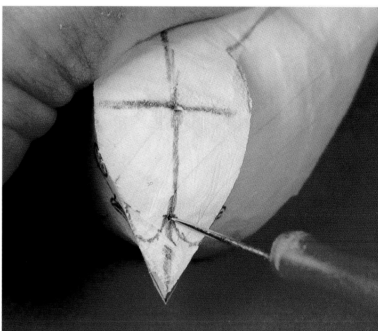

Figure 38. Measure, mark, and pinprick the 0.4 inches top beak dimension on the centerline. Draw in the v-shape at the top base of the beak.

Figure 39. With a medium pointed ruby carver, grind away the excess from the top of the beak, keeping it flat at this time. You will need to use the point of the bit to get back into the base of the v-shape. Redraw the centerline.

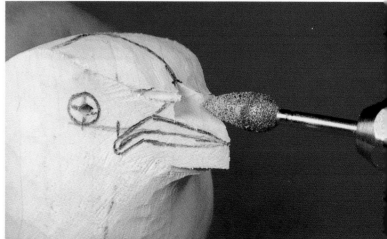

Figure 40. Cut around the sides of the beak and gape flanges and underneath. Keep the lower surface of the lower mandible flat.

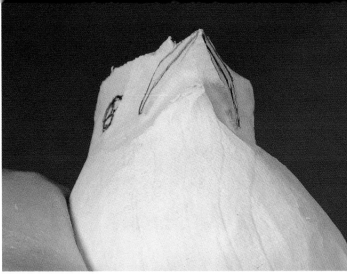

Figure 43. Round the perimeter of the little tuft of feathers under the lower mandible.

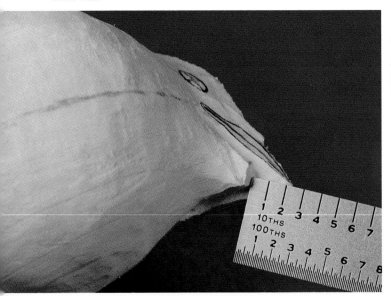

Figure 41. Cut back underneath until it measures 0.22 inches.

Figure 44. Note the difference in the shape of the top planview between the carving and study skin.

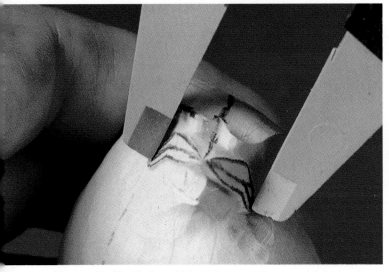

Figure 42. Check the width of the gape flanges which should measure 0.5 inches. If necessary, remove equal amounts from each side.

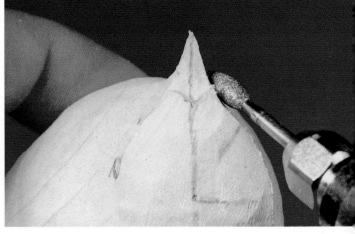

Figure 45. Remove wood from each side of the beak to give it the concave appearance of the study skin. Keep the sides of the beak straight up and down and each side balanced across the centerline.

**56 Eastern Bluebird Baby**

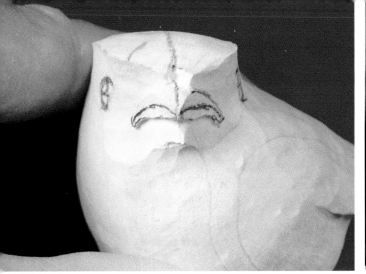

Figure 46. Redraw the commissure line. If necessary, remove a little more wood from around the outside of the beak until it protrudes from the level of the surrounding head.

Figure 49. Cut away the excess wood from the sides of the head to narrow the width of the crown. The cuts should start in the eye area and proceed to the top corner of the blank. Keep the sides of the head straight up and down--do not round yet. The cuts should not be in the ear covert area.

Figure 47. Flow the shelf under the beak down to its base. Just below the chin, remove some wood from the throat to make it concave. Round the chin and throat and blend them into the surrounding area.

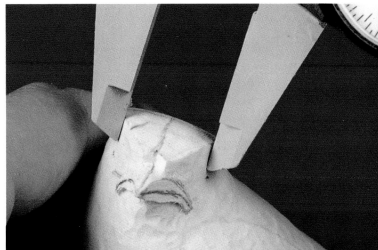

Figure 50. Keep cutting away the wood until the crown width above the eyes measures 0.65 inches. Equal amounts of wood on each side of the centerline ensure a balanced and symmetrical head.

Figure 48. On the crown, divide and mark 0.65 inches equally across the centerline above the eyes and draw in the top planview shape of the head.

Figure 51. Flow the forehead down to the base of the beak. Round the corners of the forehead, crown, and hindneck.

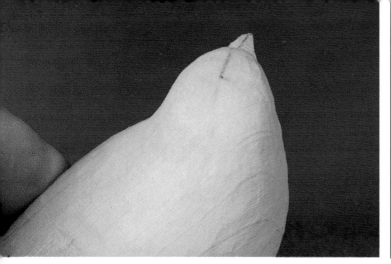

Figure 52. Flow the hindneck down onto the mantle and shoulder areas.

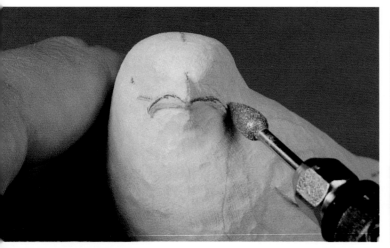

Figure 53. Round over the gape flanges on the top, rear, and bottom. Angle the front part of the beak from the top centerline down to the commissure line. Lightly round over the sharp corners on the lower mandible.

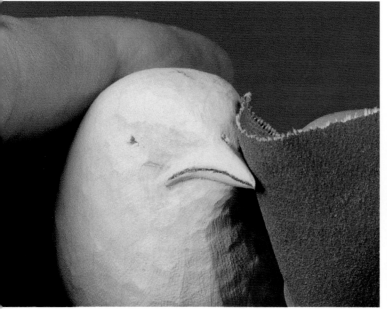

Figure 54. Lightly sand with 400 grit sandpaper. The culmen should be slightly rounded.

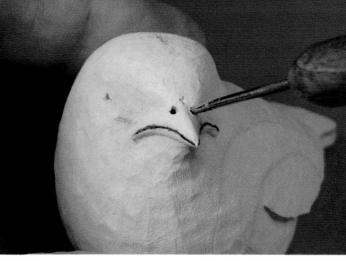

Figure 55. Mark the nostril equally on each side of the base of the upper mandible. Use a dissecting needle or pointed clay tool to press a hole at each mark. Hold the tool at a 45 degree angle to the beak's surface.

Figure 56. Check the commissure for balance from the front end view. Burn in the commissure line. The first stroke is made holding the pen perpendicular to the beak's surface and burning from the base of the gape flange to the tip. For the second stroke on each side, lay the burning pen down and burn from in front of the gape flange to the tip (the angled portion of the beak).

Figure 57. Use the tip of a sharply pointed stone to open up the burned line on the gape flanges.

Figure 58. Lightly sand the burned lines with 400 grit sandpaper. Brush or blow any dust off and saturate the beak with thin super-glue. When the glue has hardened, lightly sand with the super-fine sandpaper again to remove any hardened "nubbies".

Figure 61. Draw in the ear coverts on each side of the head making sure that they are equal in length and depth. Note that the ear covert starts at the base of the gape flange, curves down and around the back, and comes into the center of the back of the eye.

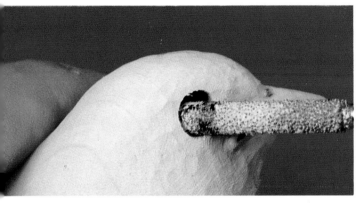

Figure 59. Recheck the eye measurements and placements. Drill 6 mm eye holes.

Figure 62. Channel around the ear covert line. Lay the ruby carver down on its side so that the point does not dig into any soft wood.

Figure 60. Check the holes for size and balance. Adjust, if necessary.

Figure 63. Flow the channel out onto the surrounding neck and throat areas. Round over the sharp edge on the ear covert itself.

Figure 64. You may need to remove a little wood below and in front of the eye to create a slight depression for it to sit in.

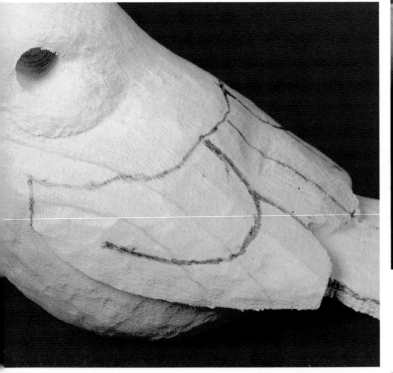

Figure 65. Measure and mark the 0.9 inches length of the mantle from the end of the primaries. Measure and mark the 0.5 inches distance from the end of the primaries and secondaries on each wing. To show the little patch of breast feathers that cover the forward portion of each wing, draw a small arc from the front of the lower wing edge upward toward the head. Draw in the mantle line from the front of the arc line on both sides and through the 0.9 inches measurement mark. Draw the inside of the tertials, go through the 0.5 inches measurement mark for the secondaries, and draw their lower edge. Draw the inside line from the primaries to the secondaries on each side.

Figure 68. Round down the edge of the mantle and side breast fluffs.

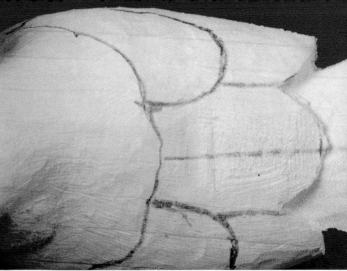

Figure 66. Note the irregular path of the mantle line.

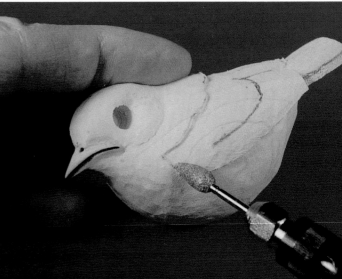

Figure 67. Laying the ruby carver down on its side, cut a light channel just behind the mantle and side breast fluff lines on each side. Flow the channel out toward the wings and thus lowering their surface. It will appear that the wings are lower and are coming out from underneath the mantle.

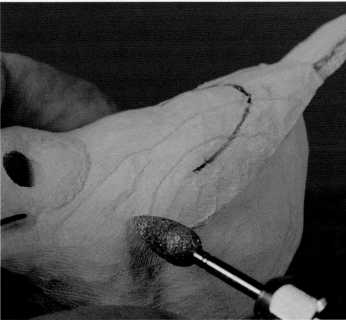

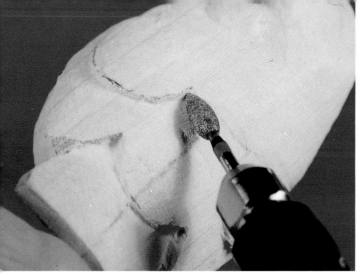

Figure 69. Cut a channel around the secondaries and the inside perimeter of the tertials on each wing. Flow the channel out onto the surrounding area of the primaries and middle of the back.

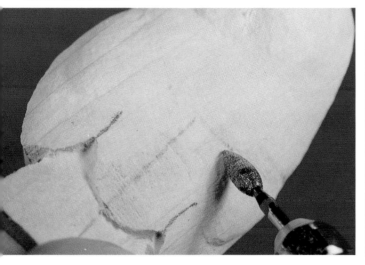

Figure 70. Round over the tertial's inside edges, tips and lower secondary edges.

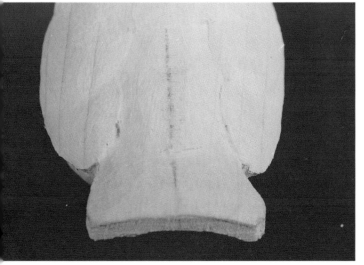

Figure 71. Cut along the inside edges of the primaries and roll down the corners of the upper tail coverts. Lightly round down the inside primary edges. Round the tips of both sets of primaries.

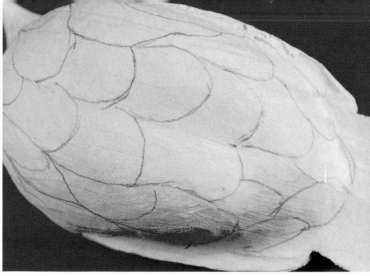

Figure 72. Draw in the varied shapes of the feather contouring. There is not just one right way for the contouring to appear. It changes each time the bird changes position or rearranges its feathers. You want the pattern to be pleasing to look at and to have an interesting flow.

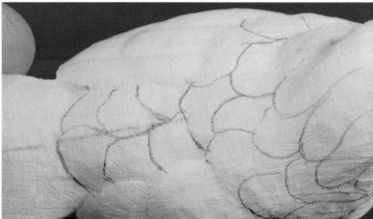

Figure 73. Draw in the contouring on the hindneck, mantle, back, and upper tail coverts.

Figure 74. Channel along each of the contouring lines.

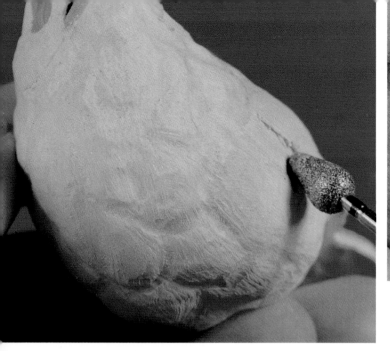

Figure 75. Round over each of the feather fluffs.

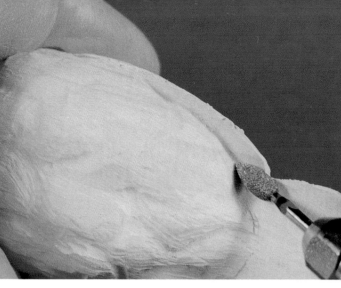

Figure 77. With a small medium pointed ruby carver, relieve the wood underneath the lower wing edges. Do not take so much wood out that the lower wing edge becomes very fragile. The actual primary edge needs to appear thin, but the wood should get thicker as it progresses into the wing.

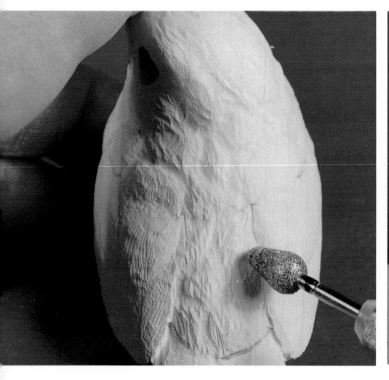

Figure 76. Make the channels a little shallower on the topside of the baby so that the feather fluffs are more subtle.

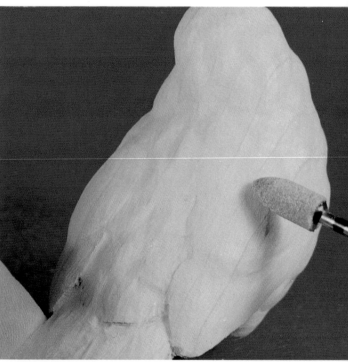

Figure 78. Smooth the entire bird (except the beak) with a large blunt pointed stone. You will need a smaller smoothing stone for some places that the large one cannot get to.

Figure 79. Layout the wing and tail feathers. The dotted lines are the quills.

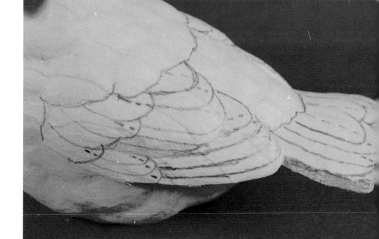

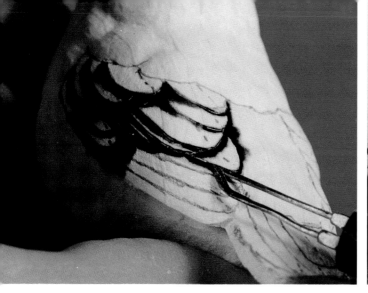

Figure 80. Laying the burning pen on its side, begin burning around each feather edge at the front of the wing and proceed back toward the rear.

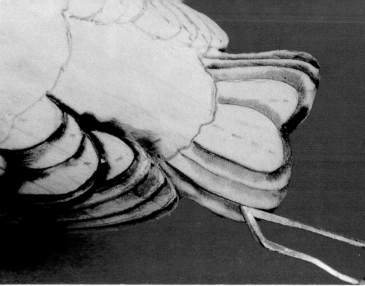

Figure 83. When you lay the pen entirely on its side, you will get a wide burn demarcation as you see here. The wide burn ensures a gradual transition to the feather below.

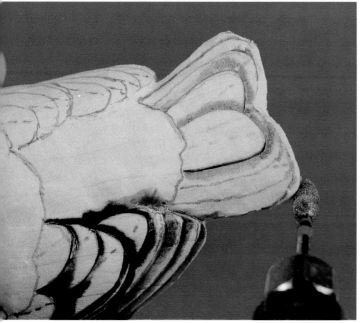

Figure 81. Grind away the excess around the tail feather tips.

Figure 84. Burning a fine line down each side of the tail edges will give the appearance of two feathers laying on top of another.

Figure 82. Thin the tail feather edges by holding the ruby carver bit at an angle. Do not remove any wood from the center of the tail, just the side edges and end. Smooth the undertail surface.

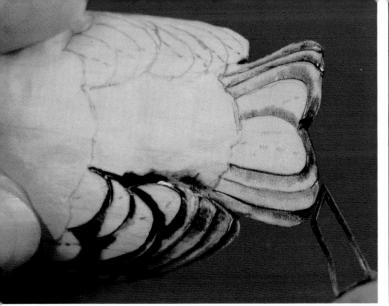

Figure 85. Burn around the end of each feather to give the position of the inner edge on the underside.

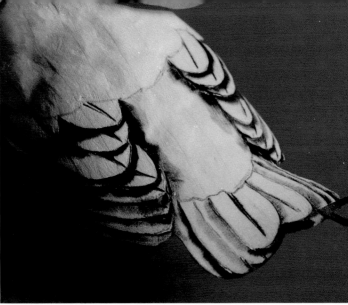

Figure 87. Burn in the quills by burning two close lines converging just short of each feather tip. On small feathers a single burn line will suffice.

Figure 86. Layout the feathers on the underside using the burned marks from the previous step. Burn in the underside edges.

Figure 88. Begin burning in the barbs by starting at the lowest primary and progressing upward and forward on the wing.

Figure 89. Place each burn stroke as close as possible to the preceding one. As you can see on the burned wing, there are no unburned areas of wood.

Figure 90. Begin burning the barbs on the tail on the outer feathers and work towards the center.

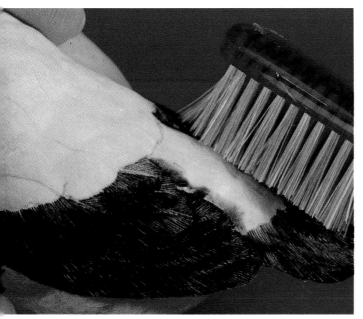

Figure 91. Clean all burning with a toothbrush to remove any carbon deposits. I prefer a natural bristle toothbrush which can be purchased from most health food stores.

Figure 92. Burn in the quills on the underside. Begin burning the barbs on the middle of the underside of the tail and proceed towards the outer feathers.

Figure 93. Burn in the quills on the underside of the primaries and then burn in the barbs. A small pointed burning pen is useful to burn in barbs in tight places.

Figure 94. Drawing in the feather shapes may help to keep the feathers from getting too small or large. Avoid fish-scale rows.

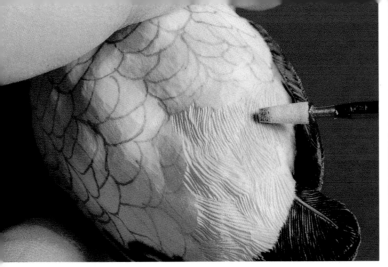

Figure 95. Begin stoning in the feather barbs on the underside at the edge of the lower tail coverts. Using a small cylindrical stone will enable you to create fluffy feather tips without obscuring the nearby areas.

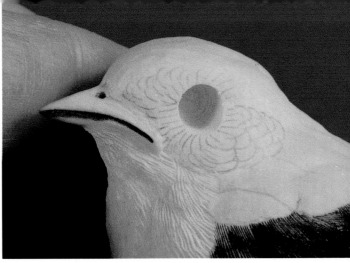

Figure 98. The feather flow pattern around the eye radiates from its edge and originates at its front center.

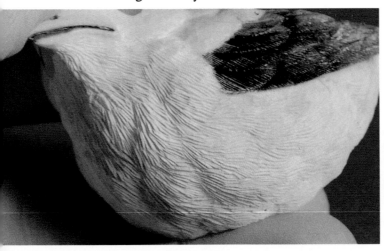

Figure 96. Proceed stoning up the underside keeping the stoning strokes as close as possible. An adjustable light at a low angle, shooting across the bird's surface will enable you to see the stoning more easily.

Figure 99. Use just the tip of the burning pen with short strokes to achieve the bristly look of the feathers around the eye. The strokes should get longer as they proceed to the rear of the ear covert.

Figure 97. Clean the stoned areas with the laboratory bristle brush on a mandrel at low speed with a light touch. Running the brush at too high speed or pressing too hard will wipe out stoning.

Figure 100. Burn up close to the underside of the beak where the stoning could not reach.

Figure 101. Draw in the feather pattern on the upper tail coverts, back, mantle, neck, and head.

Figure 102. Starting at the edge of the upper tail coverts, begin working your way up the bird towards the head. Clean all burning with the toothbrush.

Figure 103. Check the eyes for proper fit before beginning the eye setting procedure.

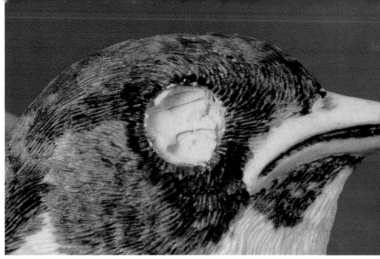

Figure 104. Fill the eye holes with the oily clay.

Figure 105. Cut the wires from the eyes as close as possible without fracturing the eye.

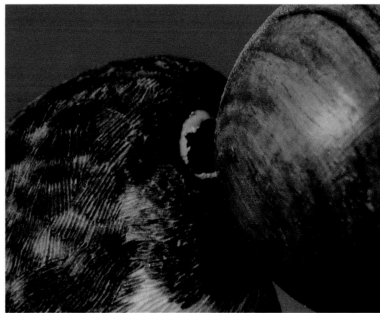

Figure 106. Use the end of a wood-handled tool to press the eyes into position.

**Eastern Bluebird Baby 67**

Figure 107. The eyes should be evenly placed, not too deep or bulging out too much.

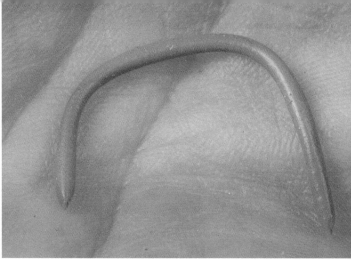

Figure 110. After kneading the putty to an even green color, roll a small worm shape.

Figure 108. Clean the excess clay from the crevice with the pointed end of a clay tool or a dissecting needle.

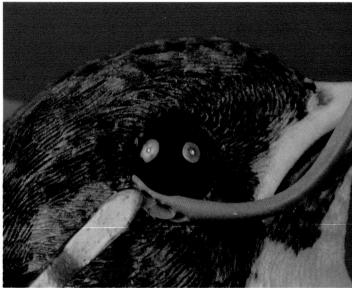

Figure 111. Press the worm down into the crevice between the eye and the edge of the hole. This is a pinching motion so that the putty will stay put. Allowing a small bead of putty to remain near the eye's surface forms the actual eye ring that is needed.

Figure 112. Work the worm down into the crevice all the way around the eye and pinch off the extra.

Figure 109. Use the toothbrush to rid the area around the eye of any clay. The putty will not stick to clay. I use a ball of clay on my bench to plunge the tool in to keep the putty from sticking to its surface while I am forming the eye ring (or any other putty procedures).

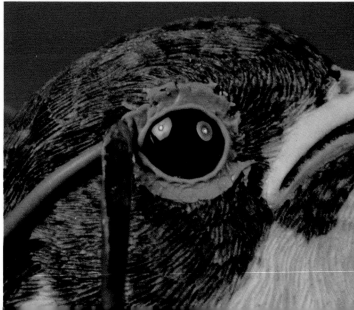

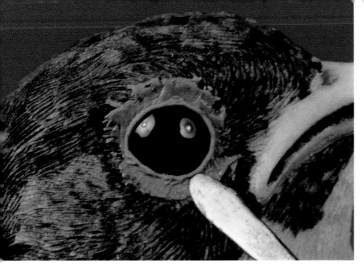

Figure 113. Make the height and thickness of the eye ring as small as possible by pressing down any excess.

Figure 116. Pull the putty into the surrounding texturing remembering the flow of the small feathers around the eye.

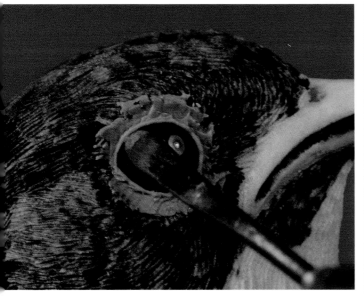

Figure 114. Shape the inside of the eye ring. Note that it is an oval shape.

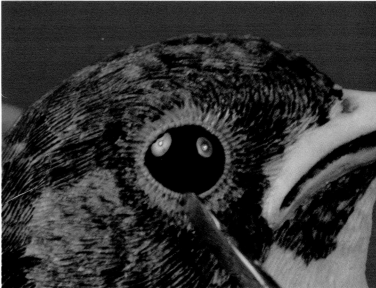

Figure 117. Put radiating lines on the actual eye ring. Allow the putty to harden.

Figure 115. Pull off the excess from around the eye. You do not need a half-inch of putty around the eye--just as little as possible to cover the crevice and blend into the surrounding texturing.

Figure 118. Hold the bird above the mount and mark the exit point of each tarsus.

Figure 119. Since a bird's legs move in many positions and directions, there is not just one placement point. Generally, the exit points will be a little forward of the vent area. Unless a bird is in some animated position (such as landing, taking off, fighting, etc.), it will be balanced over its toes.

Figure 122. Because of the position limitations of feet castings, I usually prefer to use cast toes and 16 gauge galvanized wire for the tarsus. For this little baby, only part of the tarsus will be showing. Drill the 1/16" holes at the appropriate angle and fitted the wire, leaving about 0.6 inches to go into the mount.

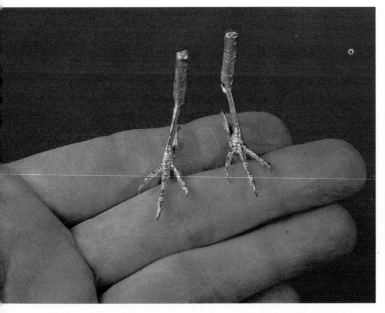

Figure 120. Here you see a pair of bluebird feet castings. The bird's left foot is on the right. Note that the hind toe comes off the inside of the tarsus.

Figure 121. To use the casting, sight the angle into the bird and drill the appropriate sized hole. Check for accuracy and glue into place.

Figure 123. Holding the bird in position over the mount, mark the placement for the wires or castings.

Figure 124. Drill holes for the wires or castings that are slightly larger than their diameters, so they can be fitted more easily.

Figure 125. Fit the bird to the mount. This may necessitate rebending the wires or castings, remembering that the tarsus is a straight bone.

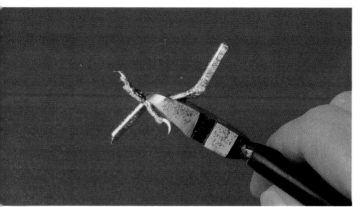

Figure 126. One way to get cast toes is to clip above and below the main toe joint on a foot casting.

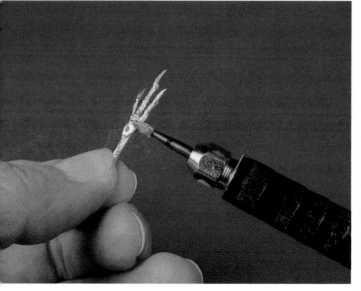

Figure 127. Carve away any excess casting material from the sides of the toes, and smooth the main toe joint. Do not use a ruby carver or diamond bit on castings, as the bits will quickly clog and be rendered useless. Use a carbide bit with cutting edges. Carefully drill 1/16" diameter holes through the meaty part of the main toe joint.

Figure 128. Fit the toes on the wires and fit the bird on its mount.

Figure 129. File light horizontal lines across the wire near the main toe joint.

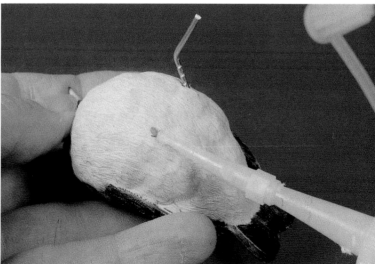

Figure 130. Put super-glue down into one hole. Quickly put the foot wire in and place the bird on its mount, checking for proper position. Do the other foot the same way.

Figure 131. Burn in the texturing underneath the lower wing edge where the stoning could not reach, and blend it into the surrounding area.

Figure 134. When the putty has hardened, spray the entire bird with Krylon Crystal Clear 1301.

Figure 132. Fit the toes on the wires and put the bird on its mount with the toes positioning properly. Use thick super-glue or 5 minute epoxy to glue the toe castings to the wire. Do not put so much glue that it runs down into the driftwood.

Figure 135. Apply undiluted gesso to the entire bird using a stiff bristle brush and a dry-brush technique. It will likely take two very thin applications. When the gesso is dry, carefully scrape the eyes.

Figure 133. Mix up some ribbon epoxy putty. Apply a small amount around the main joint at the base of the tarsus. Sometimes, the putty resists sticking to wire or metal. Heating the wire with a hair dryer helps immensely. Texture the putty at the base of the tarsus with horizontal lines. Roll a small worm of putty, and pinch and flatten it on the rear of the wire to represent the hind tendon.

**72  Eastern Bluebird Baby**

# PAINTING THE BABY BLUE BIRD

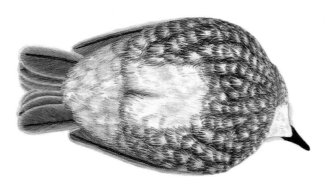

Liquitex Acrylics (jar) colors:
White = W
Payne's grey = PG
Burnt umber = BU
Raw umber = RU
Ultramarine blue = UB
Raw sienna = RS
Burnt sienna = BS
Yellow oxide = YO
Gesso
Matte and Gloss Mediums

* Indicates that a small amount should be added.

Figure 1. The centers of the feathers on the study skin's ear coverts and shoulder are light grey with darker edgings.

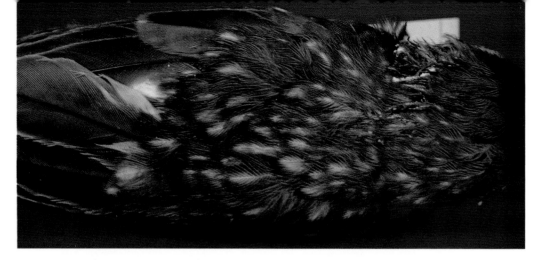

Figure 2. On the mantle, the centers of the feathers are a light grey in an arrow-shape. There is an occasional small light blue patch.

Figure 3. There is a bluish cast on all of the wing feathers.

Figure 4. Note the light edgings on the wing feathers.

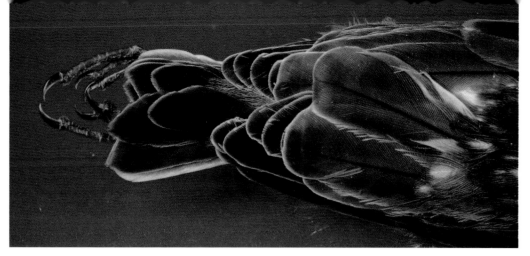

Figure 5. The dominant blue color on the wings is primarily near the quills.

Figure 6. The light centers are larger on the underside of the bluebird baby.

Figure 7. Note the light brown color of the feet. In the live bird with an adequate blood supply, the color is darker.

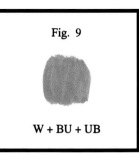

Fig. 8

BU + UB + W

Fig. 9

W + BU + UB

Figure 8. For the basecoats on the head, mantle, back, and upper tail coverts, mix burnt umber, ultramarine blue, and white to a grey. Apply several coats to cover the gesso. On the ear coverts and sides of the head, apply sparingly with a dry-brush technique. Remember that when you mix a grey, it will dry a shade darker. Apply a mixture of burnt umber and white in a wash over these same areas.

Figure 10. On the sides of the head and ear coverts, apply alternating dry dabs of the light grey and then the darker grey. Working the two colors back and forth will enhance the softness.

Figure 11. Apply a very thin burnt umber wash to the head, mantle, back, and upper tail coverts. Do the light spots again with the light grey mixture, and apply another burnt umber wash. Doing the light areas and then washing dark several times will soften the colors.

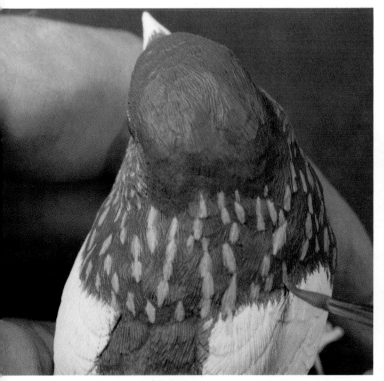

Figure 9. For the light spots on the sides of the head, the mantle, and shoulders, mix white with burnt umber and ultramarine blue to a light grey. Use a small pointed brush to paint in the arrow shapes.

**76 Eastern Bluebird Baby**

Figure 12. Add more white to the light grey mixture, and paint in the centers of all of the light shapes.

Figure 13. Blending burnt umber, ultramarine blue, and a small amount of white to a dark grey, edge the feathers on the head (top and sides) and neck.

Fig. 13

BU + UB + *W

Figure 14. Paint in very fine edgings on the mantle feathers.

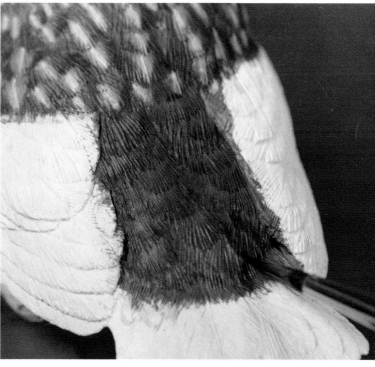

Figure 15. The dark edgings on the back and upper tail coverts are wider.

**Eastern Bluebird Baby  77**

Figure 16. Apply a super-thin raw sienna wash and then a thin ultramarine blue wash to the head, mantle, back, and upper tail coverts.

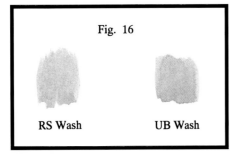

Fig. 16

RS Wash          UB Wash

Figure 17. Blending ultramarine blue with small amounts of burnt umber and white, paint a few random areas at the bases of feathers.

Figure 18. Darken the eye ring on both eyes with a mixture of burnt umber, ultramarine blue, and a small amount of white.

Figure 19. Blending white with small amounts of burnt umber and ultramarine blue to a light grey, dry-brush in the light circular pattern around the eye and the spots behind it on both sides. Apply a thin wash of a mixture of burnt umber and ultramarine blue.

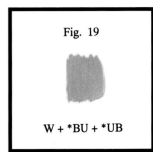

Fig. 19

W + *BU + *UB

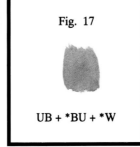

Fig. 17

UB + *BU + *W

**78  Eastern Bluebird Baby**

Figure 20. For the basecoats on the wings and upper tail surface, mix ultramarine blue, payne's grey, white, and a small amount of burnt umber. Apply several thin coats until the gesso is covered.

Fig. 20

UB + PG + W + *BU

Figure 21. Blending burnt umber, payne's grey, and a small amount of white, apply wide edgings to the feathers on the wings and tail.

Fig. 21

BU + PG + *W

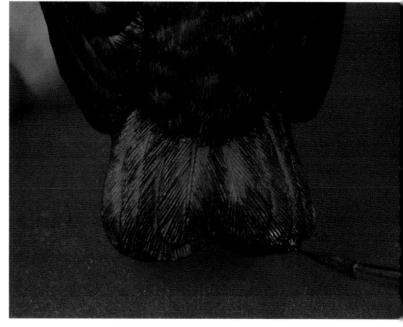

Figure 22. The secondary and outer tail feather edgings are not quite as wide as the others. Darken the quills on the wings and tail with the edging mixture.

Figure 23. Mix a large amount of water with the dark edging mix color to make a thin wash, and apply two of these washes to the wings and tail, drying in between.

Figure 24. Blend white, burnt umber, and payne's grey to a light grey. Apply wide edgings to the tertials. Add a little water to the mixture, and pull fine line edgings on the remaining wing and tail feathers with a liner brush. The paint needs to be thin enough for the brush to let go of it. If it is too thick, there will be blobs or no paint deposited at all.

Figure 25. Painting shadows around each feather edge enhances the three-dimensional effect on the wings and tail. Make a thin mixture of ultramarine blue and a small amount of burnt umber, and apply in a fine line at the base of each wing and tail feather.

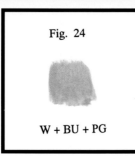

Fig. 24

W + BU + PG

Figure 26. Wash the wings and tail feathers with a thin mixture of raw sienna and a small amount of burnt umber. Do several more of these washes on the wide tertial edgings to give them a lightly rusty color.

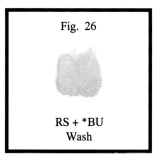

Fig. 26

RS + *BU
Wash

Figure 28. For the basecoats for the lower tail coverts, belly, breast, throat, and chin, blend white with small amounts of burnt umber, and payne's grey. Apply several thin coats of the light grey.

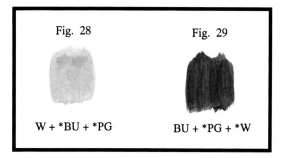

Fig. 28                          Fig. 29

W + *BU + *PG            BU + *PG + *W

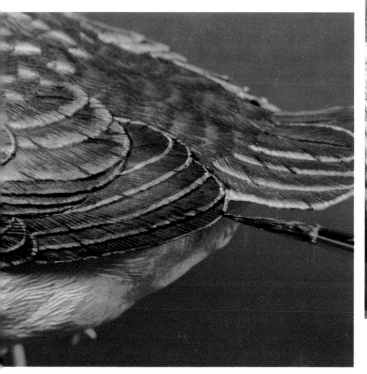

Figure 27. With a thin mixture of burnt umber and payne's grey, paint in a few random splits with a liner brush.

Figure 29. For the dark feathers edges on the underside, blend burnt umber and small amounts of payne's grey and white. Create a feather pattern over the stoned surface. Do not do any dark edges on the center of the belly. You will need to do the dark edgings several times.

Figure 30. Thin the edging mix down greatly to do the fainter edgings on the chin and lower tail coverts.

Figure 32. Mix a small amount of white into the light grey base coat mixture and pull the light center color into the dark edges. Use the light color to break up any regular patterns and to paint in splits.

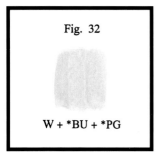

Fig. 32

W + *BU + *PG

Figure 33. Make a thin wash with the light grey color, and wash the chin and lower tail coverts.

Figure 31. Apply a very thin wash with a mixture of burnt umber, raw sienna, and white to random areas on the breast and flanks.

Figure 34. Blend burnt umber, ultramarine blue, and white to a medium grey, and apply several basecoats to the underside of the tail and under the lower wing edges. Be careful that the paint does not track around the feather edges to the topside.

Fig. 34

BU + UB + W

Figure 35. Apply a thin wash of a mixture of ultramarine blue and a small amount of white to the undersides of the wings and tail. When this is dry, apply a thin mixture of white with small amounts of burnt umber and ultramarine blue in fine line edgings on the edge of the wing and all of tail feathers.

Figure 36. Wash the underside of the tail and wings with a super-thin mixture of white and burnt umber.

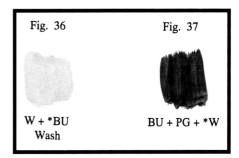

Fig. 36

Fig. 37

W + *BU
Wash

BU + PG + *W

Figure 37. Coat the entire beak several times with a mixture of burnt umber, payne's grey, and a small amount of white.

**Eastern Bluebird Baby 83**

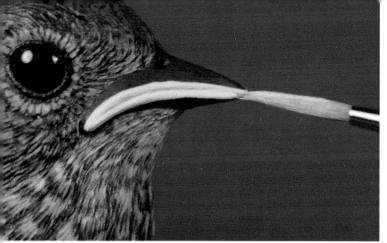

Figure 38. For the yellowish band above and below the commissure line, apply a mixture of white, yellow oxide, and a small amount of raw umber. The band is slightly wider back on the gape flanges than out on the tip. It will take several coats to cover the dark color.

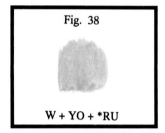

Fig. 38

W + YO + *RU

Figure 39. Make a wash out of the beak's dark basecoat mix, and apply an overall wash to the beak. When this is dry, apply several more to the yellowish band near the beak's tip, drying in between. Use thinned burnt umber and a liner brush to pull a fine line down the commissure.

Figure 41. Use a mixture of burnt umber and a small amount of payne's grey to darken the claws. Water down the claw mixture, and apply an overall wash to the tarsi and toes.

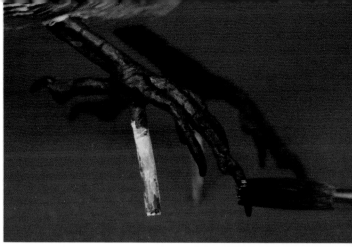

Fig. 41

BU + *PG

Figure 42. Coat the beak with an equal mixture of matte and gloss mediums.

Fig. 40

BU + BS + *W

Figure 40. For the basecoats on the tarsi and toes, blend burnt umber, burnt sienna, and a small amount of white, and apply several thin coats.

Figure 43. Mix a small amount of gloss medium in a large amount of water, and coat the feet. When this is dry, apply undiluted gloss to the claws and quills. Carefully scrape the eyes and glue the baby on its perch.

Figure 44. The completed bluebird baby!

# Chapter 4

# Bobwhite Quail Chicks

## *(Colinus virginianus)*

One October several years ago, Betsy Cameron brought me four newly hatched quail chicks. It was so much fun raising these little "guys" at my house. I had a large cage I had built that was their home for many months. It was such a joy to raise them. In the morning, when I would be in the kitchen fixing Jenna's lunch for school, they would whistle their "bob-white" call to me. That call became a favorite sound to me. Sometimes the quail would be in the shop with me while I worked on birds. Sometimes I had them in the living room. Because they were born late in the season and the winter months here in Delaware can be very cold, they had to stay put with me until warm weather. In April of that year when the weather finally warmed, I released them. It had been a marvelous experience, one that I have not forgotten!

Since quail are so afraid of people, their nests are hardly ever seen unless abandoned. Most of what is known about their nests and babies comes from people actually raising them. In the wild, the nest is located on the ground under low cover near open spaces such as fields or meadows. It usually is in a depression in the ground and may be haphazardly constructed with small twigs, grasses, and weeds. The female usually lays 12-16 dull creamy white eggs, which she incubates the eggs about 24 days. The chicks normally hatch within an hour of one another. The young babies are born covered with down and are up running about shortly. The parents lead the young away from the nest within twenty-four hours. Both parents brood and care for the young, teaching them how to feed and how to avoid danger. Within two weeks, the young quail have sufficient flight feathers to manage short flights.

## DIMENSION CHART

1. End of tail to end of winglet: 0.7 inches
2. Length of winglet: 0.6 inches
3. End of tail to front of winglet: 1.3 inches
4. End of tail to upper tail coverts: 0.2 inches
5. End of tail to lower tail coverts: 0.2 inches
6. End of tail to vent: 0.5 inches
7. Head width at ear coverts: 0.8 inches
8. Head width above eyes: 0.55 inches
9. End of beak to back of head: 0.95 inches
10. Beak length
    top: 0.25 inches
    center: 0.3 inches
    bottom: 0.2 inches
11. Beak height at base: 0.21 inches
12. Beak to center of eye: 0.5 inches, 4 mm brown eyes
13. Beak width at base: 0.25 inches
14. Tarsus length: 0.5 inches
15. Toe lengths
    inner: 0.4 inches
    middle: 0.6 inches
    outer: 0.45 inches
    hind: 0.25 inches
16. Overall body width: 1.2 inches
17. Overall body length: 2.0 inches

## TOOLS AND MATERIALS

Bandsaw (or coping saw)
Flexible shaft machine
Carbide bits
Ruby carvers and/or diamond bits
Knives, chisels, and v-tool if using basswood
Variety of mounted stones
Pointed clay tool or dissecting needle
Compass (the kind used to draw circles)
Ruler measuring in tenths of an inch
Calipers measuring in tenths of an inch
Rheostat burning machine
Awl
400 Grit sandpaper
Drill and drill bits
Laboratory bristle brush on a mandrel
Needle-nose pliers and wire cutters
Toothbrush
Safety glasses and dustmask
Super-glue and 5 minute epoxy
Oily clay (brand names Plasticene or Plastilena)
Duro ribbon epoxy putty (blue and yellow variety)
Krylon Crystal Clear 1301 Spray
Pair of brown 4 mm eyes
Tupelo or basswood block: 1.5" (H) x 1.2" (W) x 2.0" (L)
16 Gauge galvanized wire
Carbon paper
16 Gauge, 18 gauge, and 20 gauge copper wire
Small triangular file
Solder, flux, and soldering pen or gun
Permanent ink marker
Hammer and small anvil
Small block of scrap wood and staples (or several pairs of helping hands holding jigs)
Straight-jawed vise grips

# CARVING THE BOBWHITE QUAIL CHICKS

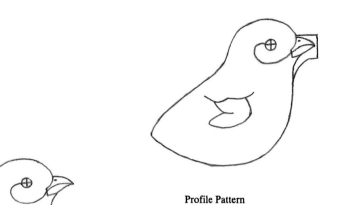

Profile Pattern

Top Plainview of Head

Profile View of Head

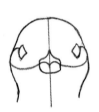

Head-on View

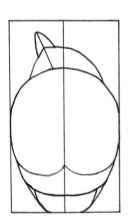

Foot

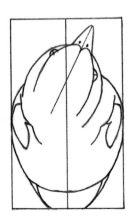

Under Plainview *

Top Plainview *

\* Foreshortening may cause distortions on plainviews.
  Check the dimension chart.

Figure 1. A covey of quail chicks seemed a bit much, so I decided that two on a small base would do nicely.

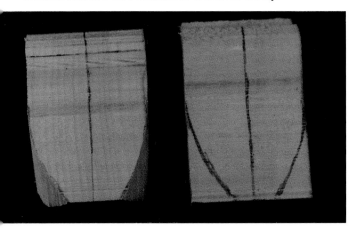

Figure 2. Transfer the profile pattern to the block of tupelo or basswood. I had a nice piece of basswood for these two chickies. Cut out the chick or chicks with a bandsaw or coping saw. Draw in the centerlines except for the beak. Using the top planview pattern as reference, draw in the body shape. Saw or carve away the excess outside of the lines.

Figure 3. Draw a centerline on the flanks from the base of the neck to the tail.

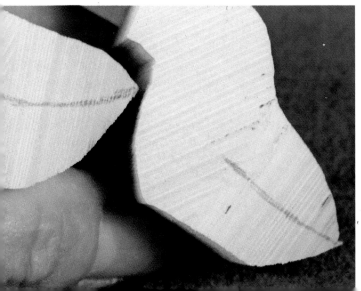

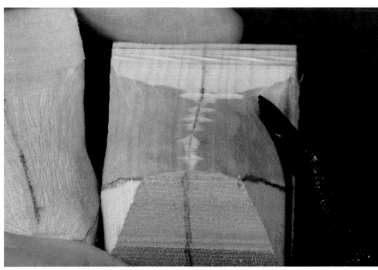

Figure 4. Round the top part of the body from the top centerline to the ones on the flanks.

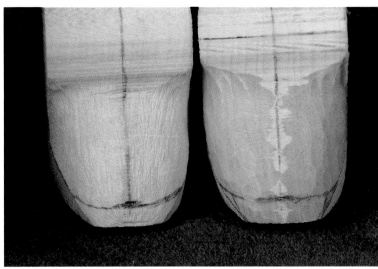

Figure 5. Measure and mark 0.2 inches from the end of the tail and draw in the upper tail covert shape.

Figure 6. Measure and mark 0.2 inches from the end of the tail on the underside and draw in the lower tail coverts. Measure and mark 0.5 inches from the end of the tail and draw in the "baby bottom" shape of the vent.

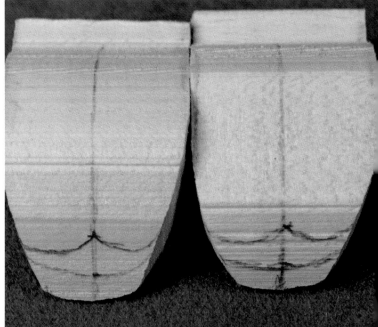

Figure 7. With a v-tool, cut around the edge of the upper tail coverts, leaving a small ledge. The small amount of tail sticking out should go straight in towards the body.

     Since I am using basswood that carves so easily, I am using some hand tools and some power tools. Either type works well on basswood. I find that power tools work better on tupelo. If you are using tupelo, you will have to substitute whatever bit will accomplish the step.

Figure 8. Roll down the edge of the upper tail coverts so that there is no shelf remaining.

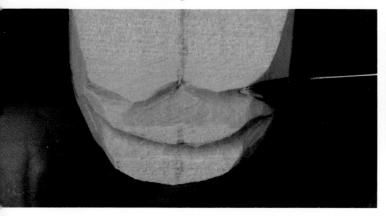

Figure 9. Cut around the lower tail covert line on the underside. Create a ledge around the vent by carving in a channel.

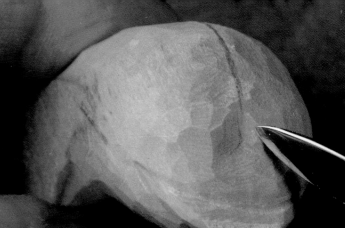

Figure 10. Shape the tail to a blunt point. Flow the lower tail coverts down to the base of the tail. Round over the vent area down to the lower tail coverts. Round the belly from the underside centerline to the ones on each flank.

Figure 11. For the nestled down chickie, just round the flanks. Do not round all the way to the centerline on the flat plane.

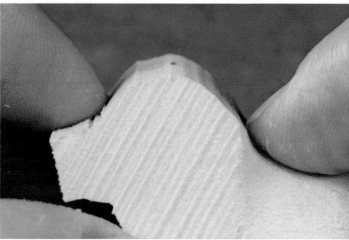

Figure 12. Find the center of the head by placing one finger at the base of the beak and one finger about half-way down the back of the neck. Optically choose and mark the midway point.

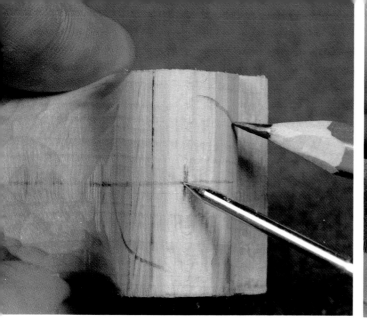

Figure 13. Set the point of the compass lightly at the head midpoint and the pencil at the base of the beak. Swing an arc of that dimension to the side to which you want the head to turn. Turn the compass to the opposite back quadrant of the head, and swing an arc with that same dimension.

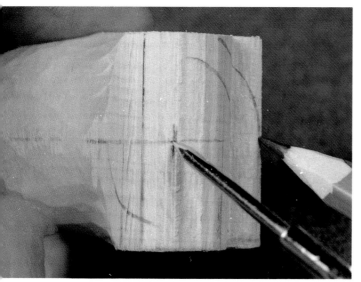

Figure 14. Change the compass dimension to the distance between the midpoint to the end of the beak. Swing an arc of that dimension to the head turn side.

Figure 16. The widest part of the bird's head is the width between the ear coverts. Holding a ruler perpendicular to the new centerline, measure and mark 0.8 inches (0.4 inches on each side of the centerline).

Figure 17. Looking straight down on the top of the head, roughly draw in the planview shape of the head, encompassing the measurement marks. The wood outside of the lines is waste wood.

Figure 15. Using a ruler, draw a new head centerline that intersects all three arcs and passes through the pivot point. It is helpful to erase the old centerline.

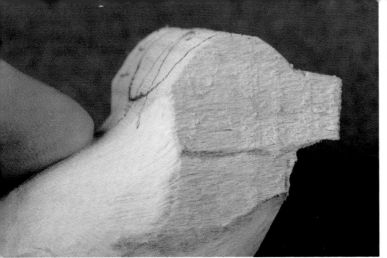

Figure 18. Draw a line the depth of the head on each side from underneath the beak to the back of the head. When cutting away waste wood, do not go below this line.

Figure 19. Cut away the excess wood from around the head on its sides and in front of the beak. Do not remove any wood from the back of the head yet. Keep the sides of the head and beak straight up and down.

Figure 20. Keep equal amounts of wood on each side of the centerline. Check the measurement of the head width at the ear coverts with the calipers.

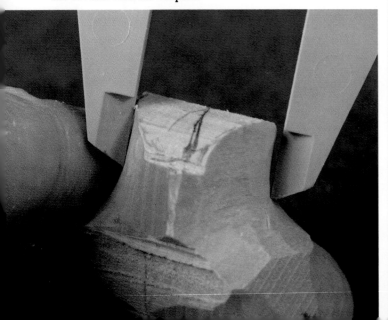

Figure 21. You may need to use a smaller bit to snug up to the line along the sides of the beak.

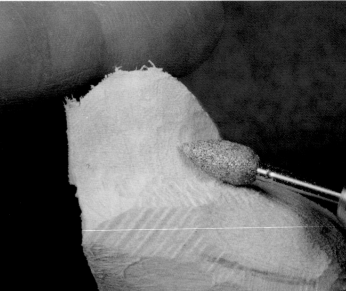

Figure 22. Use a smooth ruby carver to get rid of the deep scratches made by the carbide cutter. It is difficult to draw accurate lines over rough terrain.

Figure 23. Flow the head down to the shoulder and side breast areas, getting rid of the shelf.

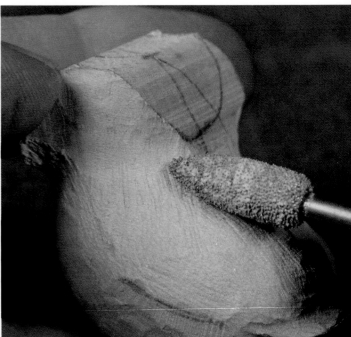

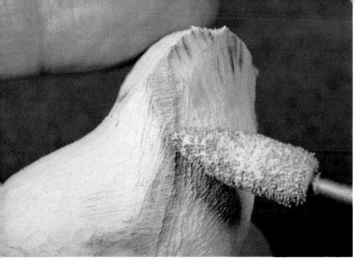

Figure 24. Round the breast from the sides to the centerline.

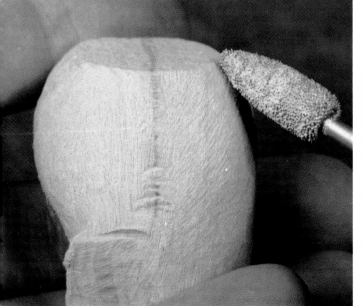

Figure 25. On the nestled down chickie, flow the breast into the rounded flanks. There should still be a flat plane on the belly.

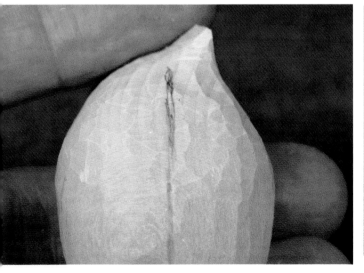

Figure 26. Failure to round the breast all the way to the centerline will leave the bird too square.

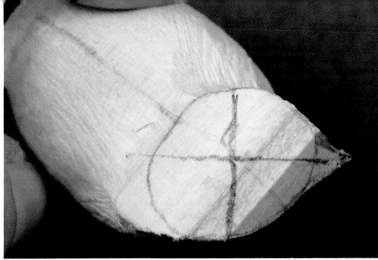

Figure 27. On the top of the head, draw a line perpendicular to the centerline and through the pivot point, dividing the head into quadrants.

Figure 28. On the forehead, the high quadrant is the one on the same side as the head turn. The high quadrant on the back of the head and neck is on the opposite side.

Figure 29. Cut away the excess on the high forehead side so that it equals the other side. The further the head turn, the more wood you will need to cut away.

Figure 30. Even up the quadrants on the back of the head and neck. Flow the hindneck out onto the mantle and shoulder areas.

Figure 33. There is a small tuft of feathers at the base of the underside.

Figure 31. Note the profile shape of the beak of a quail chick mount.

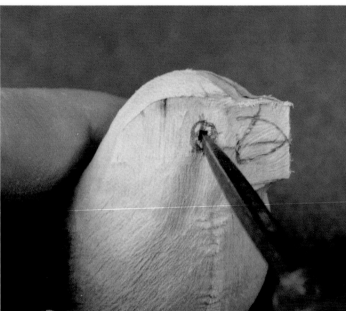

Figure 34. Transfer the beak and eye placements from the profile pattern to the blank. Check all positions with a ruler. Mark the eye centers deeply with an awl. The commissure line is actually curved, but can be drawn straight at this point.

Figure 35. Lightly pinprick the base of the beak at the commissure line and bottom of lower mandible.

Figure 32. The forehead feathers protrude out onto the sides of the beak to form a modified v-shape.

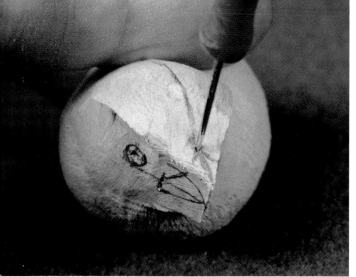

Figure 36. Measure, mark, and pinprick the top beak length (0.25 inches) on the centerline. Draw in the v-shape with the point of the "v" at the pinprick.

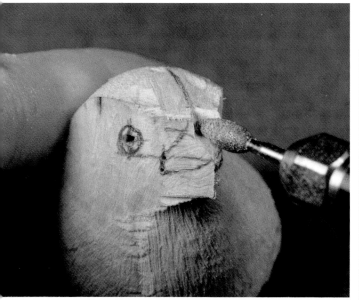

Figure 37. Use a small medium pointed ruby carver to grind away the excess on the top of the upper mandible and back into the v-shape. Keep the top of the upper mandible flat with this cut.

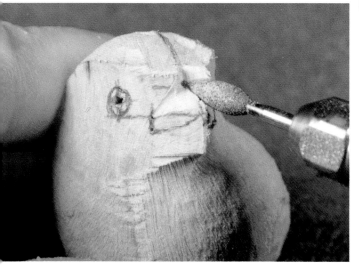

Figure 38. Redraw the top centerline. Angle the upper mandible from the top centerline to the commissure line. Do not undercut the little curved tufts of feathers that lay on each side of the upper mandible at its base.

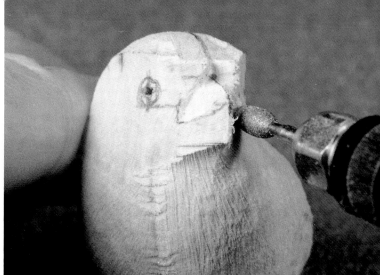

Figure 39. To get the proper width at the base of the beak, begin cutting inside the lower mandible lines on each side. Keep checking for beak balance from the front end view to make sure there are equal amounts of wood on each side of the centerline (culmen). It is important to keep the sides of beak (lower mandible) straight up and down.

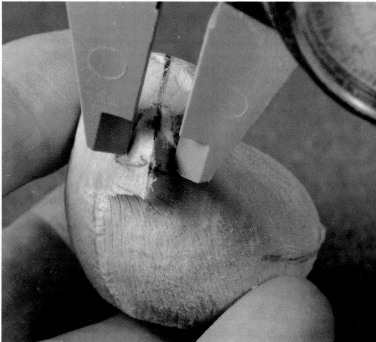

Figure 40. Keep cutting away the sides until the calipers measure 0.25 inches.

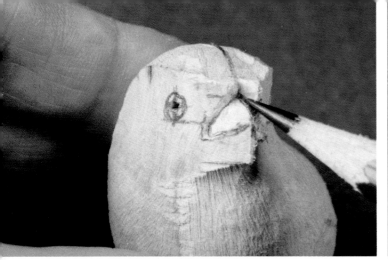

Figure 41. Use a sharpened pencil to redraw the lines inside of the cuts on the top and sides of the beak. Snug the line right up into the corners.

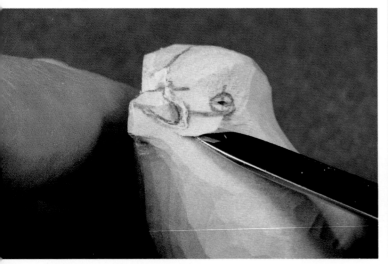

Figure 42. Flow the sides of head down to the base of the beak. The cuts will start gradually at the eye placements and proceed down to the pencil line, but do not cut into the beak. There should be no shelf remaining on the sides of the beak.

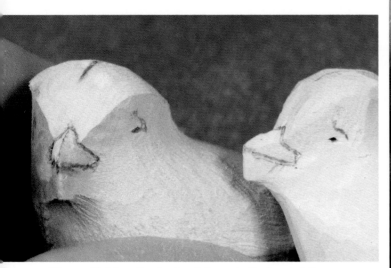

Figure 43. Flow the forehead down to the base of the upper mandible maintaining the existing plane. There should be no shelf left on the top of the beak, even at the "v". Do not round the corners yet.

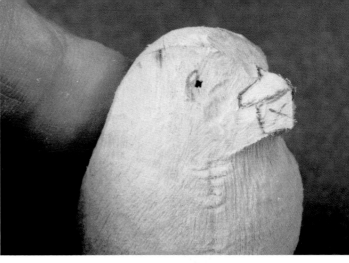

Figure 44. Measure and mark 0.2 inches from the tip of the beak on the sides and underneath.

Figure 45. Cut away the excess under the beak back to the mark. Keep the bottom of the beak flat.

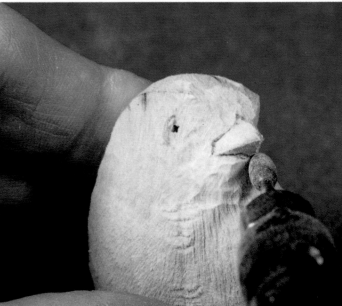

Figure 46. Round the edges of the little tuft around the sides. Flow the shelf down to the base of the beak.

Figure 47. Scoop out some wood from the chin to give it a concave shape. The chin and throat should be rounded over.

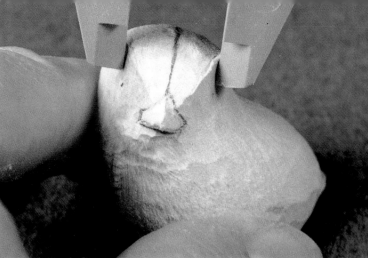

Figure 50. Keep equal amounts of wood across the centerline. Check the dimension with the calipers.

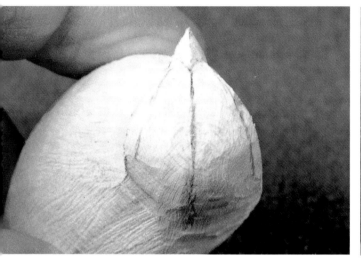

Figure 48. Measure and mark 0.55 inches equally across the centerline on the crown above the eyes. Draw the wedge shape of the head encompassing the marks. Make sure that the eye centers are pinpricked deeply so that their positions are maintained even with wood removal.

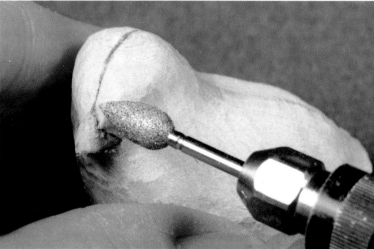

Figure 51. Round the forehead, crown, and hindneck.

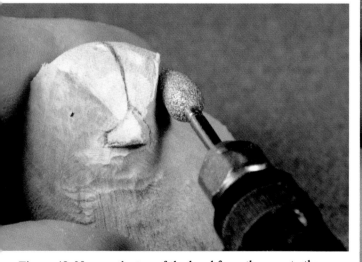

Figure 49. Narrow the top of the head from the eyes to the corner of the blank. Keep the sides of the head straight up and down and do not round yet.

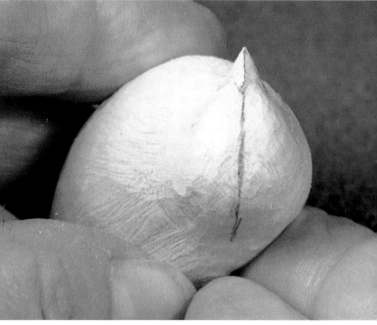

Figure 52. Flow the hindneck onto the mantle and shoulder areas.

**Bobwhite Quail Chicks  97**

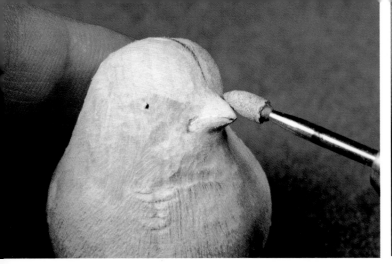

Figure 53. Sand the beak or use a stone to smooth its contours, rounding over the culmen and corners of the lower mandible.

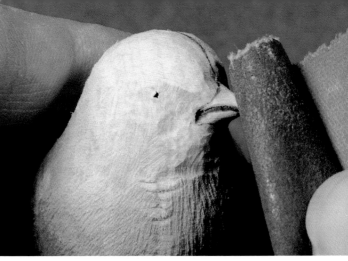

Figure 56. Lightly sand the beak with 400 grit paper.

Figure 54. Redraw the curved commissure line and burn it in with the pen held vertically to the beak's surface.

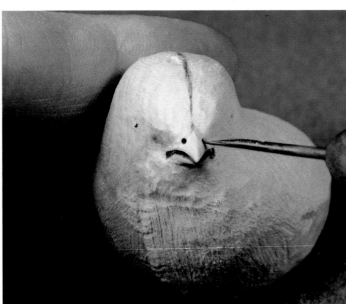

Figure 57. Mark the nostrils equally on each side of the upper mandible. Press in the nostrils with the pointed end of a clay tool or dissecting needle held at an angle.

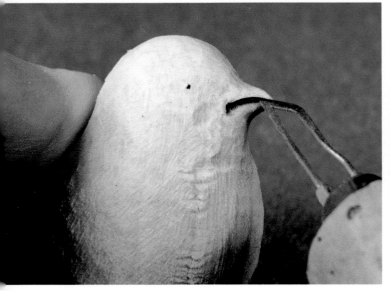

Figure 55. Laying the burning pen down on its side, burn up to the first burn line.

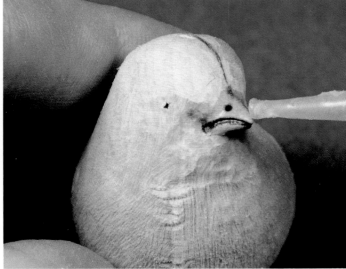

Figure 58. Saturate the beak with thin super-glue. When the glue has hardened, fine sand again.

**98  Bobwhite Quail Chicks**

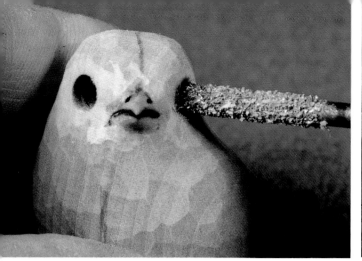

Figure 59. Recheck the eye positions and drill 4 mm eye holes, making sure that they are balanced.

Figure 60. Check the eyes and holes for proper fit and depth.

Figure 61. Draw in the ear coverts making sure that they are the same depth and length. With a small medium pointed ruby carver, cut a channel around the ear coverts.

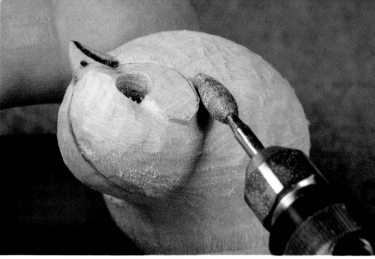

Figure 62. Flow the ear covert channel out onto the surrounding neck and throat.

Figure 63. Round over the sharp edge on the ear covert. You may need to remove a small amount of wood under and in front of the eye to create a depression for it to sit in.

Figure 64. Transfer the winglet positions to the carving. Clear acetate, sold in most large art stores or through their catalogs, is helpful in transferring patterns and their parts to carvings. Use a permanent marker to trace the patterns on the acetate, hold it over the carving, put the pencil under the acetate, and mark the particulars. You may have to make some adjustments since the drawing is two dimensions and the carving is three. Always check dimensions with a ruler.

**Bobwhite Quail Chicks 99**

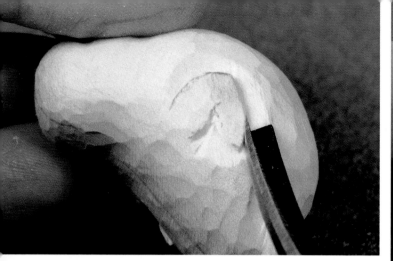

Figure 65. Raise the winglet from the surrounding area by cutting around its edges.

Figure 66. Flow the cut out onto the flank and back, and round over the winglet's sharp edges.

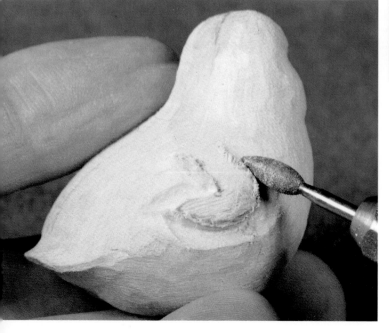

Figure 67. If you are power carving, channel around the winglet, flow the channel out onto the surrounding area, and round over the edges.

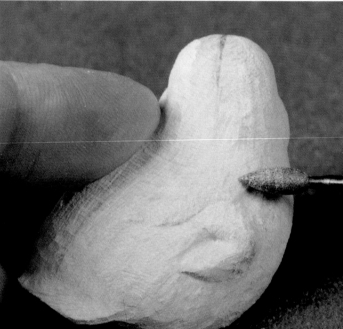

Figure 68. Draw in the scapular fluffs above the winglets. Cut a channel underneath the fluff, lowering the upper winglet section (actually the bird's forearm).

Figure 69. Flow the channel out and round over the sharp edge of the scapular fluff.

**100 Bobwhite Quail Chicks**

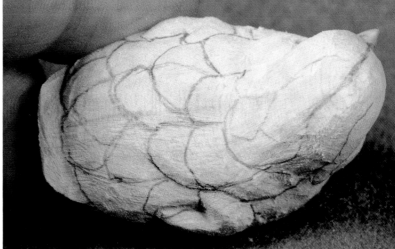

Figure 72. To create the clumps of down, draw in interesting shaped contours on the hindneck and back.

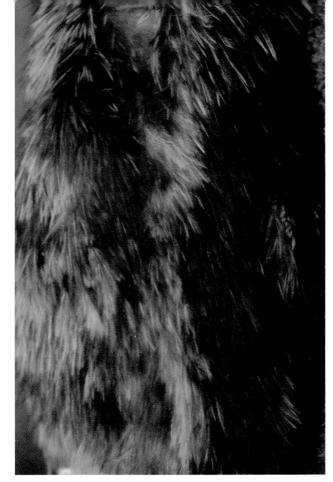

Figure 70. On the topside of the quail chick study skin, you can see the clumps of down.

Figure 71. The underside of the quail chick.

Figure 73. Also draw in the clump on the underside of the bird.

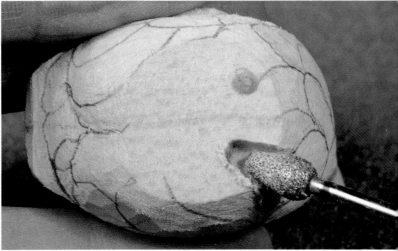

Figure 74. On the nestled down chick, mark the toe insertion placements. With a blunt pointed ruby carver, cut a blunt v-shaped channel to hold the toes. Carve the channel so the toes will be pointed slightly outward on both sides.

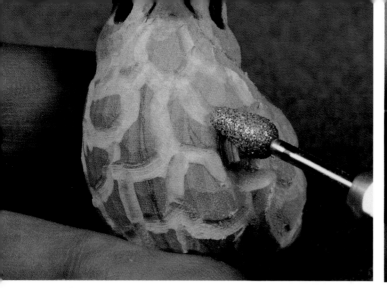

Figure 75. Cut the channels for the down fluffs with the blunt pointed ruby carver.

Figure 78. Stone the entire bird except the beak.

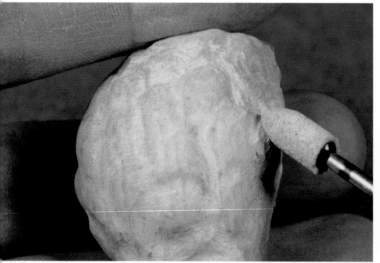

Figure 76. Round over each of the clumps.

Figure 79. Stone the underside beginning with the tail and working forward to the base of the beak.

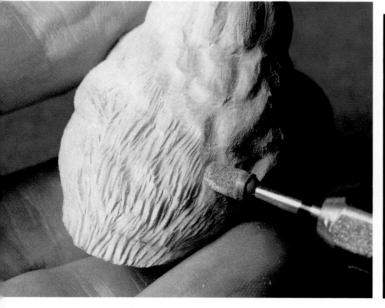

Figure 77. Starting at the tail and working forward, stone grooves of various depths in the clumps.

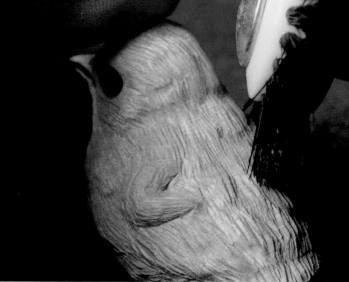

Figure 80. Clean any fuzz off with the laboratory bristle brush on a mandrel running at low speed.

Figure 81. Begin burning in the down at the base of the beak and work backward to the tail. By burning from front to back, you use each stroke of the burning pen to determine the length of the stroke in front of it. Each stroke should be slightly deeper at the beginning. Pull up gradually so that there is lighter pressure at the end of the stroke. This burning technique is call indent burning.

Figure 84. The burning strokes are longer on the back.

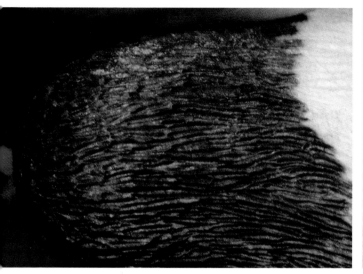

Figure 82. The down is very short near the beak and gets progressively longer as you work your way back on the head.

Figure 85. On the underside, start burning at the chin and proceed back towards the tail. The strokes are short near the beak and get longer back on the body.

Figure 83. On the winglets, the down flows down the forearm, makes its turn at the wrist, and flows back to the tip.

Figure 86. On the nestled down baby, you do not need to burn the flat plane where the bird will sit.

Figure 87. Cleaning the burned areas with a toothbrush will rid the surface of any carbon deposits.

Figure 88. Drill 1/16" diameter holes one-half inch deep into the toe channels of the nestled down bird.

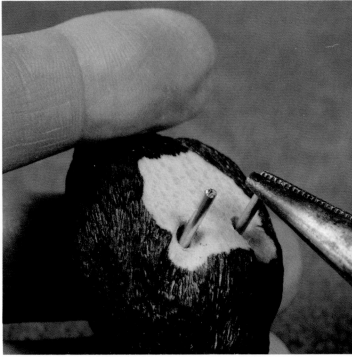

Figure 89. Fit and glue pieces of 16 gauge galvanized wire into the holes leaving about one-half inch protruding.

**104 Bobwhite Quail Chicks**

Figure 90. Holding the chick above the ground material, mark the wire placements. Drill 5/64" diameter holes into the ground. Put the bird wires down into the holes and check for a proper fit.

Figure 91. Put a piece of carbon paper on the base with the carbon side up to the bird.

Figure 92. Scrunching the bird down on the carbon should leave bits of carbon on the bottom of the bird where the high spots are.

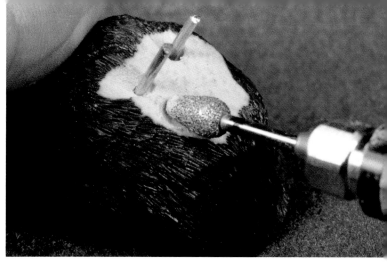

Figure 93. Cut away the high spots. Keep marking the bottom of the bird and removing the high spots until there is a good fit of the bird and ground.

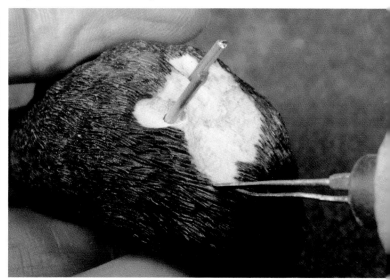

Figure 94. Burn the outer edges of the chick's belly that might show.

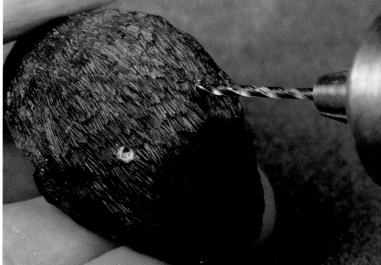

Figure 95. For the standing chick, mark the exit placements of the tarsi. The bird should be balanced over its toes. Drill 1/16" diameter holes one-half inch deep into the belly.

Figure 96. Fit 16 gauge galvanized wire into the holes. Mark the ankle joint at the body, and measure and mark the tarsus length (0.5 inches). Leave about 5/8" of wire to go into the mount or ground.

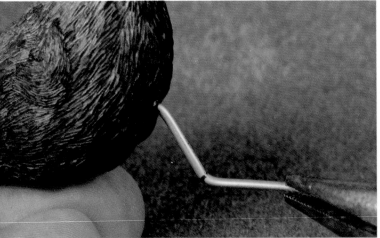

Figure 97. Make the appropriate bends so that the bird will be balanced over its toes.

Figure 99. Fit the wires into the holes and check for balance and position. Adjust the bends of the wires if necessary.

Figure 100. Check the birds' positions from all angles.

Figure 98. Hold in place and mark the entrance points. Drill 5/64" diameter holes into the ground or mount.

Figure 101. Note the toes on the foot of the quail mount.

Figure 104. Flatten each of the claws on an anvil.

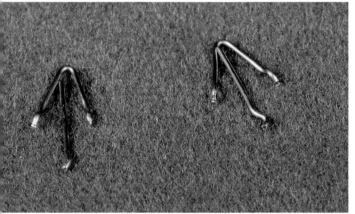

Figure 102. On the nestled down bird, you will only need the forward three toes. Using 18 gauge copper wire, measure 0.4 inches (inner toe), make a sharp bend in the wire, and then measure and cut the wire at the 0.45 inches mark (outer toe). Place this wire with the slightly shorter sided inner toe on the left of your workbench (left set of toes). Do another bent wire the same dimensions, flip it over, and place on the right side of your bench (keep this one as the right set of toes). Cut two wires each 0.6 inches long and place one with each set of toes.

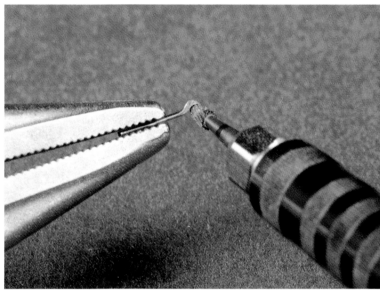

Figure 105. Shape the claws with a carbide cutter.

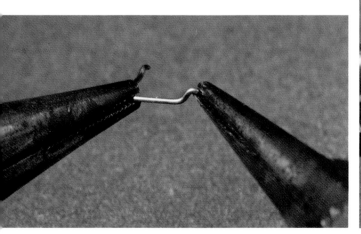

Figure 103. Use a small pair of needle-nosed pliers to bend the claws.

Figure 106. File the scale markings on each of the toes. Sand lightly.

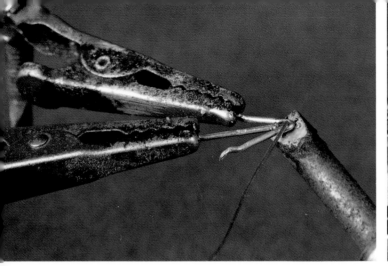

Figure 107. Holding the inner/outer claw combination and the middle toe in place stapled on a block of wood or held in position with helping hands holding clamps, flux and solder the main toe joint.

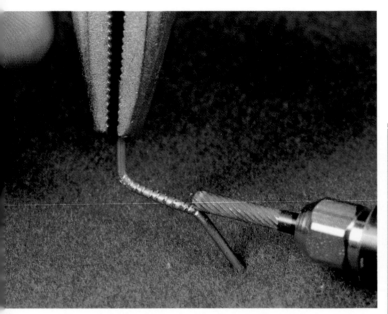

Figure 108. With a file or square-edged carbide cutter, make the lines on the tarsus wires of the upright chick.

Figure 109. Lightly sand the markings to remove any burrs.

Figure 110. Bend and create the markings on the forward toes as you did for the nestled down bird. For the hind toe/hind tendon combination, measure and mark 0.25 inches on a piece of 20 gauge copper wire. Bend the wire at the measurement mark and shorten it to the tarsus length. Fashion the claw and file the scale markings on the hind toe. Fit the mount end of the wire into a scrap block of wood. Hold the forward toes in place with staples or jigs. Use a small alligator clamp to hold the hind toe/hind tendon wire in place. Flux and solder the main toe joint and the hind tendon.

It is amazing how little time it takes me to write about making feet and how long it actually takes me to do it!!

Figure 111. Place the upright bird in place and check the toes for fit. You may have to bend them up or down to fit the mount. Leave a small space between the toes and the mount for the toe pads.

Figure 112. Mix a small amount of the ribbon epoxy putty. Roll a small worm.

Figure 113. Cut off a small section of the worm and apply it to the bottom of one of the toes. Heating the wire with a hair dryer for a few seconds helps the putty stick to the it. Texture along the sides and bottom of the pads. Anytime the putty sticks to the tool, push it into a ball of the oily clay. The oil coating prevents the putty from sticking.

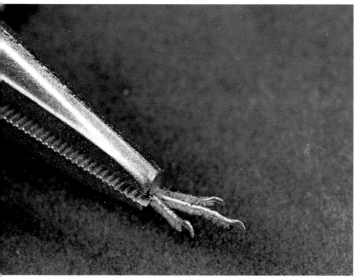

Figure 114. Do the remainder of the toes. The pads should be slightly wider than each toe.

Figure 115. For the feet on the upright bird, do the toe pads, and then apply a small amount of putty at the main toe joint, making horizontal lines to simulate the wrinkling.

Figure 116. There is a small short web at the base of the toes. Put a small amount of putty there and texture in some wrinkles.

Figure 117. Put the feet in the bird and the bird in place on the mount and check for proper fit.

Figure 118. Remove one foot, place super-glue in the hole, replace the foot, and quickly put the bird back in place on the mount. Adjust the bird and foot position quickly before the super-glue dries. Glue the other foot the same way.

Figure 119. When the glue has dried, apply a small amount of putty at the body/foot junction for the leg tuft. Apply hair-like texturing strokes to the leg tufts and allow to harden.

Figure 122. Continue setting the eyes according to the directions at Figure 104 in the Bluebird Chapter page 67. Allow the putty to harden.

Figure 120. On the nestled down bird, do not glue the toes in place. Put the toes in place to check for proper fit, but wait to glue them in place until the toes and bird are completely painted.

Figure 123. Spray both birds with Krylon Crystal Clear 1301.

Figure 124. Apply several coats of gesso dry-brushed with a stiff bristle brush to the entire bird. When dry, carefully scrape the gesso from the eyes.

Figure 121. Fill the eye holes with oily clay, cut the eyes from the wires, and press them into place. They should not be too deep or too shallow.

# PAINTING THE BOBWHITE QUAIL CHICKS

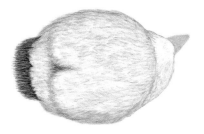

Liquitex Acrylics (jar) colors:
White = W
Payne's grey = PG
Unbleached titanium white = UBW
Burnt umber = BU
Raw umber = RU
Burnt sienna = BS
Raw sienna = RS
Yellow oxide = YO
Gesso
Matte and Gloss Mediums

* Indicates that a small amount should be added.

Figure 1. The profile view of the quail chick's head.

Figure 2. The planview of the head.

Figure 3. Note the dark and light stripes on the back.

Figure 4. There is a gradual transition at the shoulder area between the darker colors on the back and the lighter ones of the breast.

Figure 5. The lighter colored down on the quail chick's underside.

Figure 6. The dark down is sometimes visible underneath.

Figure 7. Blending burnt sienna, burnt umber, and a small amount of yellow oxide to a rusty brown, apply several basecoats to the v-shape on the top of the head, scapular fluffs, middle of the back, and tail.

Figure 8. Also apply the rusty colored basecoat to the edge of the tail underneath.

Figure 9. Blend burnt umber and small amounts of payne's grey and white to a medium grey-brown, and apply to the head, shoulders, winglets, back, and flanks. It will take several applications to cover the gesso.

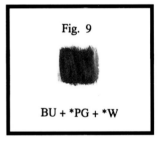

Fig. 9

BU + *PG + *W

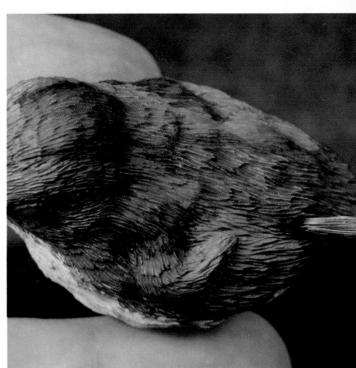

Figure 11. Dry-brush in the dark stripes on the outer perimeter of the v-shapes on the head and back with a mixture of burnt umber and payne's grey. Apply the dark color to the dark striped area behind the eye and ear coverts and random deep areas of the texturing in the rusty colored areas. Lightly darken around the eye.

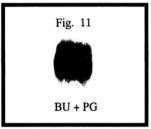

Fig. 11

BU + PG

Figure 10. Keeping the edges irregular will make it easier to blend in adjacent colors.

Figure 12. Lightly dry-brush spots and short irregular bars randomly over entire top surface of the bird.

**114 Bobwhite Quail Chicks**

Figure 13. Blending unbleached titanium white with a small amount of yellow oxide, lightly dry-brush random highlights on the entire top surface of the bird, including the tip of the tail.

Fig. 13

UBW + *YO

Figure 14. Apply a thin wash of a mixture of burnt sienna and raw sienna to the rusty colored v-shapes. On the dark stripes, apply a burnt umber wash. On the side of head, neck, and flanks, apply a raw sienna wash. Put the washes on one right after another and blend the transition areas where they meet. Then, use a hair dryer to dry them.

Repeat the dark spots and irregular barring, light highlights, and washes several times to soften all of the colors.

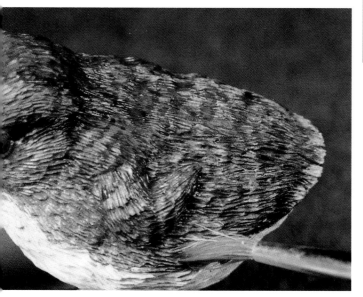

Figure 15. Blending unbleached titanium white with a small amount of yellow oxide to a creamy white, lightly dry-brush the whitish stripes outside of the dark ones on the head and neck and inside of the dark ones on the back.

Figure 16. Apply a super-thin raw sienna wash to the entire topside of the chick.

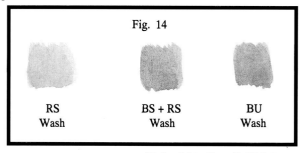

Fig. 14

| RS | BS + RS | BU |
| Wash | Wash | Wash |

Figure 17. Darken the eye rings with burnt umber and carefully scrape the eyes.

Figure 18. Apply several coats of unbleached titanium white to the underside.

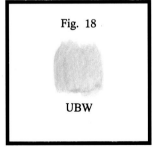

Fig. 18

UBW

Figure 19. Blend the shoulders and flank areas so that there is a soft transition.

Figure 20. Apply a thin burnt umber wash to the entire underside.

**116  Bobwhite Quail Chicks**

Figure 21. Lightly dry-brush straight white on the ends of the texturing on the downy clumps.

Figure 22. Apply the white more solidly in the chin area.

Fig. 24

W + *RU
Wash

Figure 23. Apply a very thin white wash to the entire underside of the bird.

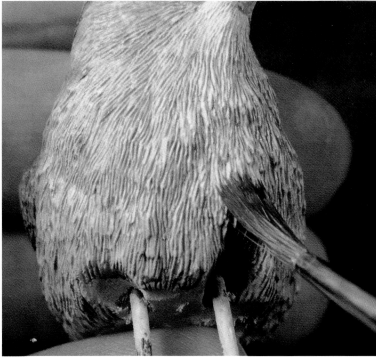

Figure 24. When the white wash is dry, apply a thin wash of a mixture of white with a small amount of raw umber. While this wash is still wet, work in thinned burnt umber along the flanks and across the breast.

**Bobwhite Quail Chicks 117**

Figure 25. Apply a thin raw sienna wash along the shoulders and flanks.

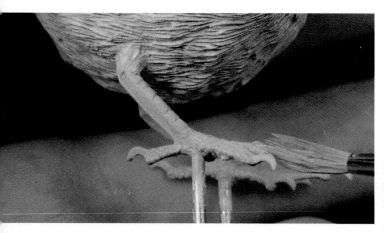

Figure 26. Blending burnt sienna with small amounts of raw sienna and white to a flesh color, apply several basecoats to the tarsi and toes.

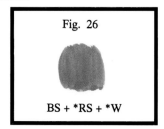

Fig. 26

BS + *RS + *W

Figure 27. Apply a thin burnt umber wash to the tarsi and toes. When this is dry, put another dark wash on the toes.

Figure 28. Blending unbleached titanium white and a small amount of burnt sienna to a light flesh color, apply several basecoats to the beak.

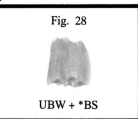

Fig. 28

UBW + *BS

Figure 29. Apply a thinned mixture of burnt umber and raw sienna to the upper mandible a hair-line above the commissure. When this is dry, darken the nostrils and the beak's tip with an additional application.

Figure 30. With a fine liner brush, darken the commissure line with burnt umber. When this is dry, apply a raw sienna wash to the entire beak.

Figure 31. Apply a mixture of equal amounts of matte and gloss mediums to the beak.

Figure 32. Mix a small amount of gloss medium in a large puddle of water and apply to the tarsi and toes. When this is dry, apply undiluted gloss to the claws. Glue the chick or chicks to their mount.

Figure 33. The completed bobwhite quail chicks!

# Chapter 5

# Killdeer Chick

## *(Charadrius vociferus)*

Several times killdeer have nested just off the road in front of my house. Since the parents incubate the eggs for approximately 24 days, I had plenty of time to observe their behavior. Most of my time during those three plus weeks was spent keeping the neighborhood kids from disturbing the parents and eggs.

Killdeer nests are usually no more than a depression on short turf or bare stony ground. Occasionally, they are lined with soft grasses. Usually, there are 4 (sometimes 3 or 5) light beige eggs with black or blackish-brown spots, streaks, or blotches. Both parents tend the eggs, incubating and turning them.

Soon after the eggs hatch, the young birds can walk and feed themselves. The parents lead the birds away from the nest within 24 hours. The fledglings fly approximately 40 days after hatching.

The young killdeer only have one black neckband, unlike the adult bird that has two. The crown and the back of the chick is mottled grey-beige and blackish-brown. There is an irregular blackish-brown stripe down the center of the back, one on the upper part of the winglet, one over the forehead and eye, and one down each flank. The tail is irregularly barred with grey-beige and blackish-brown.

## DIMENSION CHART

1. End of tail to end of winglet: 1.2 inches
2. Length of winglet: 0.6 inches
3. End of tail to front of winglet: 1.8 inches
4. Tail length overall: 0.9 inches
5. End of tail to upper tail coverts: 0.4 inches
6. End of tail to lower tail coverts: 0.2 inches
7. End of tail to vent: 1.0 inches
8. Head width at ear coverts: 0.8 inches
9. Head width above eyes: 0.6 inches
10. End of beak to back of head: 1.26 inches
11. Beak length
      top: 0.35 inches
      center: 0.45 inches
      bottom: 0.25 inches
12. Beak height at base: 0.18 inches
13. Beak to center of eye: 0.75 inches, 5 mm brown eyes
14. Beak width at base: 0.22 inches
15. Tarsus length: 0.9 inches
16. Toe lengths
      inner: 0.6 inches
      middle: 0.85 inches
      outer: 0.65 inches
17. Overall body width: 1.35 inches
18. Overall body length: 3.1 inches

## TOOLS AND MATERIALS

Bandsaw (or coping saw)
Flexible shaft machine
Carbide bits
Ruby carvers and/or diamond bits
Variety of mounted stones
Pointed clay tool or dissecting needle
Compass (the kind used to draw circles)
Ruler measuring in tenths of an inch
Calipers measuring in tenths of an inch
Rheostat burning machine
Awl
400 Grit sandpaper
Drill and drill bits
Laboratory bristle brush on a mandrel
Needle-nose pliers and wire cutters
Toothbrush
Safety glasses and dustmask
Super-glue and 5 minute epoxy
Oily clay (brand names Plasticene or Plastilena)
Duro ribbon epoxy putty (blue and yellow variety)
Krylon Crystal Clear 1301 Spray
Pair of brown 5 mm eyes
Tupelo or basswood block: 2.0" (H) x 1.5" (W) x 3.1" (L)
16 Gauge galvanized wire
16 Gauge copper wire
Small triangular file
Solder, flux, and soldering pen or gun
Permanent ink marker
Hammer and small anvil
Several pairs of helping hands holding jigs
Straight-jawed vise grip pliers
0.5 mm mechanical pencil with the lead removed

# Killdeer Chick

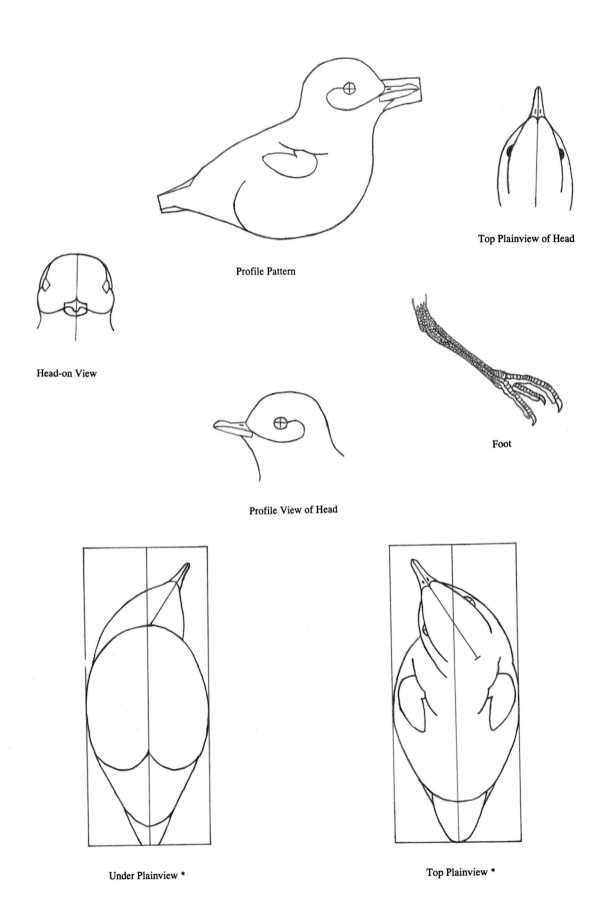

Profile Pattern

Top Plainview of Head

Head-on View

Profile View of Head

Foot

Under Plainview *

Top Plainview *

* Foreshortening may cause distortions on plainviews.
  Check the dimension chart.

Figure 1. Parent killdeer getting ready to settle in on the eggs.

Figure 3. The nest in a graveled yard of a substation was extraordinarily difficult to locate. No, the bird did not lay quarters, no matter how hard I pleaded! Note that the points of the eggs are toward the center of the depression so that the eggs do not roll away.

Figure 2. If anyone got too close to the nest, one of the parents would do its distraction display to get the intruder away from the nest.

Figure 4. Since killdeer are often found on stony terrain, I wanted this composition to include rocks. After I had collected a dozen interesting looking stones, I hot-glued them together in a pleasing arrangement to use as a model for the base.

Figure 7. The underside did not need completing since it is not seen.

Figure 5. The bird would sit atop the pile and the composition "read" well from every viewpoint.

Figure 6. I used the real rock pile to make a pattern, cut it out of one piece of basswood, and started subtracting wood until the individual shapes became apparent. When the shaping was completed, I covered the surface with modeling paste stippled in place with a stiff bristle brush. When the modeling paste had hardened, I randomly sanded any "nubbies" off and painted each stone, making each color slightly more vivid than the real rocks.

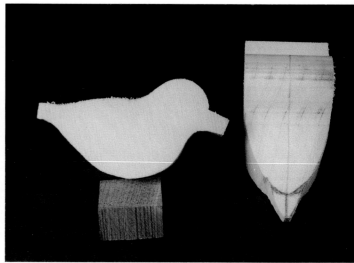

Figure 8. Transfer the profile pattern to the block of tupelo. Cut the chickie out of the block with a bandsaw or coping saw. Draw the centerlines around the bird except for the beak. Using the top planview pattern as reference, transfer or draw in the body shape, upper tail coverts, and tail. Use a ruler and planview drawings or the dimension chart to check that the drawing on the blank is correct. Bandsaw or cut away the excess from around the body and tail.

Figure 9. Using a medium pointed ruby carver, cut around the upper tail coverts and slightly round down the side edges of the tail, giving it a convex shape.

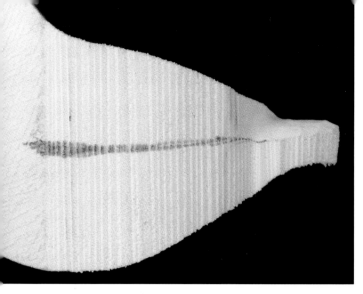

Figure 10. Draw a centerline on each flank so that it ends at the same level as the top of the tail's side edge.

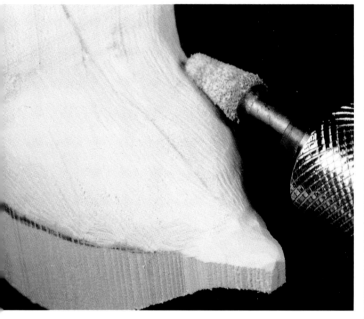

Figure 11. Round over the top of the body from the side centerlines to the top one. Roll the upper tail coverts down to the tail, eliminating the shelf.

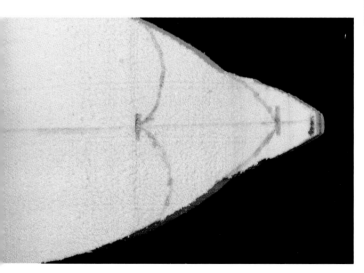

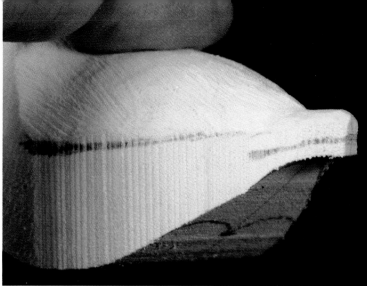

Figure 13. On the sides and end of the tail, draw a line 0.1 inches from top edge. The wood between the top edge of the tail and the line is the actual tail. The wood below the line is waste wood.

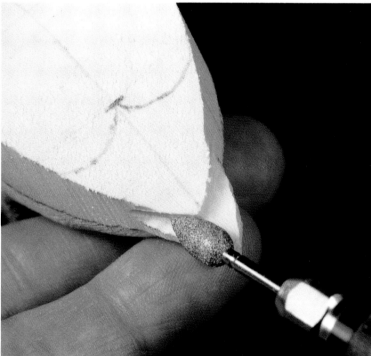

Figure 14. On the underside, use a pointed ruby carver to cut away the excess under the tail up to the edge of the lower tail coverts. The underside of the tail should be concave to correspond to the convex shape on top.

Figure 12. On the underside centerline, measure and mark the length of the lower tail coverts (0.2 inches) and the vent (1.0 inches), both measurements from the end of the tail. Draw in the v-shape of the lower tail coverts encompassing that mark and the baby bottom shape of the vent encompassing that mark.

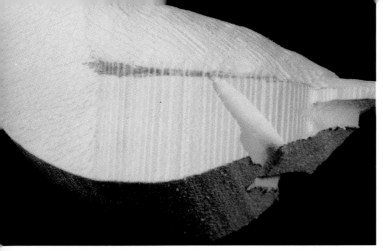

Figure 15. Using a small tapered carbide cutter, channel around the vent lines and make a shallow channel on each flank, gradually coming out of the wood as it approaches the flank centerline. The channel will need to be its deepest at the corners of the blank.

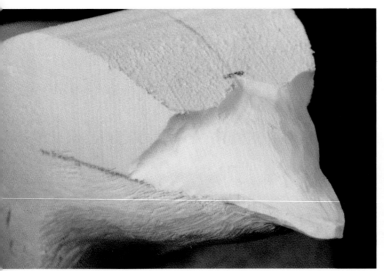

Figure 16. Round over the lower tail coverts and flow the ledge down to the base of the tail.

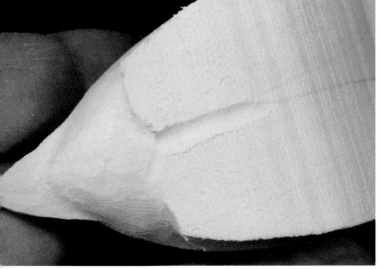

Figure 17. On the centerline at the vent, carve in a shallow channel 0.75 inches up the belly.

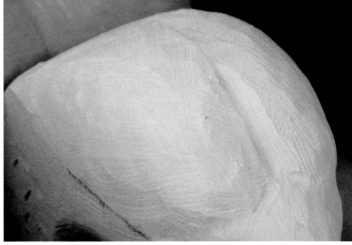

Figure 18. Round over the flanks and belly, and flow the vent ledges down to the front of the lower tail coverts. Flow the belly down into the shallow channel on the centerline.

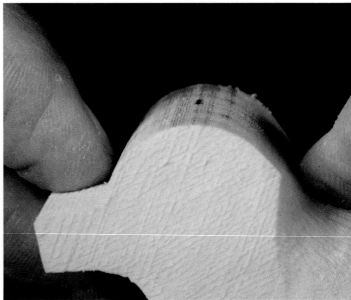

Figure 19. Find the center of the head by placing one finger at the base of the beak and another finger at the back of the head about half-way down the back of the neck. Optically determine the half-way point and mark on the head centerline.

Figure 20. Place the point of the compass at the midpoint and the pencil end at the base of the beak. Swing an arc of that dimension to the side to which you want the head to turn.

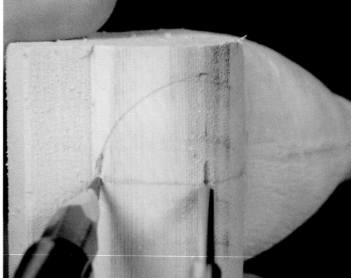

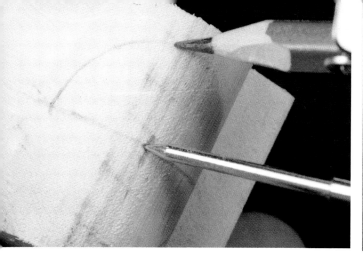

Figure 21. Turn the compass to the opposite back of the head, and swing an arc of that same dimension.

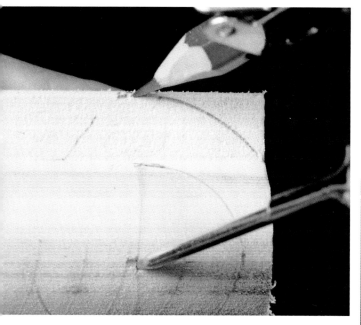

Figure 22. Lengthen the dimension of the compass to that of the end of the beak length. Swing an arc to the same side as the head turn.

Figure 23. Using a ruler, draw a new centerline that intersects all three arcs and passes through the pivot point. It is helpful to erase the old centerline.

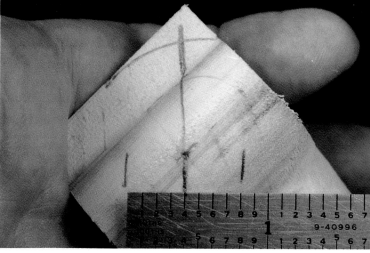

Figure 24. Hold the ruler perpendicular to the new centerline. Measure and mark 0.8 inches (0.4 inches on each side of the line). The widest part of any bird's head is the width at the ear coverts, which is 0.8 inches on the killdeer chick.

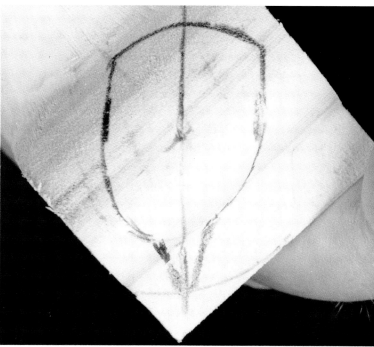

Figure 25. Looking straight down onto the top of the head, draw in the planview head and beak shape encompassing the measurement marks. You do not need to do any beak measurements. Just draw it oversized.

Figure 26. On the sides of the head, draw a line from underneath the beak towards the back of the head. When cutting away the waste wood from the head, do not cut below this line.

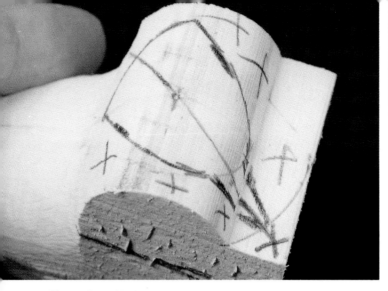

Figure 27. All of the wood around the planview lines is waste wood.

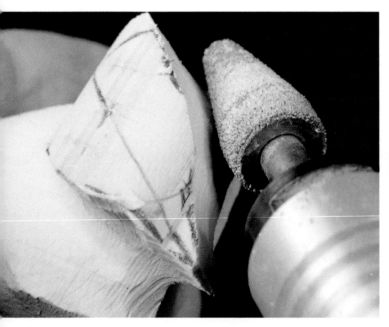

Figure 28. Using a medium tapered carbide cutter, cut away the excess wood from around the head, keeping the sides of the head and beak straight up and down. When you start getting close to the lines, make sure that there are equal amounts of wood on each side of the centerline to keep the head balanced. Do not remove any wood from the back of the head yet.

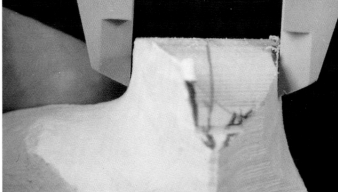

Figure 30. Check the 0.8 inches measurement with the calipers.

Figure 31. Flow the shelf on the head turn side out onto the shoulder and side breast areas.

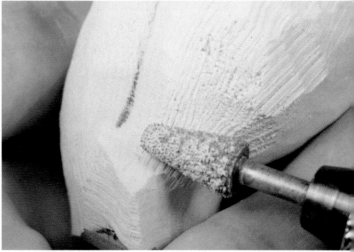

Figure 32. Round the breast from the sides to the centerline on the throat. Do not remove any wood from the underside of the beak.

Figure 29. You may need a small bit to work in close to the beak. Use the ruby carver to smooth away any deep scratches made by the carbide cutter. It is difficult to draw accurately on a rough surface.

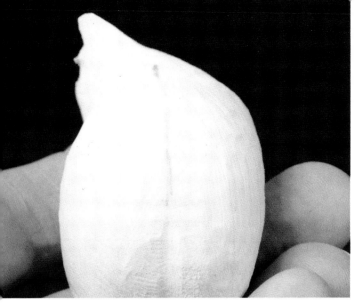

Figure 33. Rounding over the breast all the way to the centerline will ensure that there are no flat spots. Do not leave the chick square-chested.

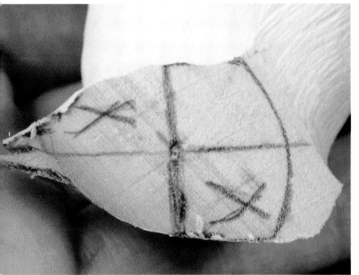

Figure 34. When you cut the profile pattern out as the blank and then turn the head of the bird in the wood, the planes on the top of the head are at a strange angle. If you hold the bird in a natural position and look at the bird's head straight on, you can see that the top of the head is weird. To fix this, you have to even up the high areas. On the top of the head, draw a line perpendicular to the centerline at the pivot point, which will divide the head into quadrants. On the forehead, the high area is on the quadrant on the same side as the head turn.

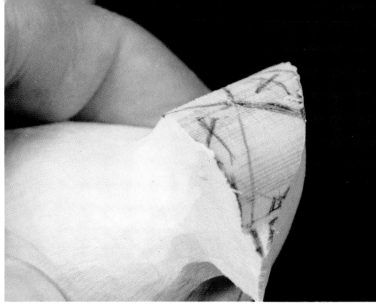

Figure 35. The high spot on the back of the head and neck is on the opposite side.

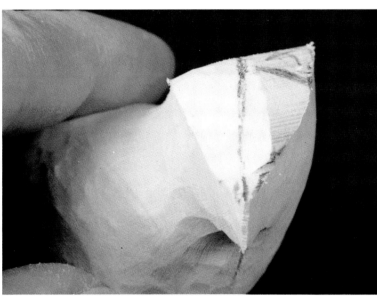

Figure 36. Cut the high area off the forehead quadrant so that its surface matches the other side. Sometimes, you will need to cut past the centerline or quadrant line to even up the surface. You may need to cut away any high areas on the head turn side of the beak as well. The more the head is turned, the more wood you will need to remove. If you have to cut away the centerline, redraw it as soon as possible.

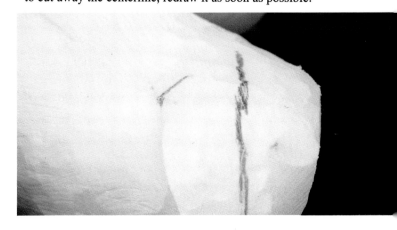

Figure 37. Whack off the high areas on the back of the head and neck. Flow the hindneck down onto the mantle and shoulder areas.

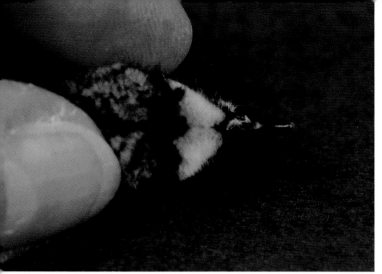

Figure 38. The top planview of a killdeer chick's beak.

Figure 39. The profile view.

Figure 40. The bottom planview.

Figure 41. Transfer the beak and eye placements from the profile pattern. Check the positions with a ruler. Make sure that they are even on each side from the front end view. Deeply pinprick the eye centers and lightly pinprick the commissure line and bottom of lower mandible at the base of the beak.

Figure 42. Measure, mark, and lightly pinprick the top beak length (0.35 inches). Draw in the v-shape of the upper mandible.

Figure 43. Using a medium pointed ruby carver, begin carving away the excess above the upper mandible back into the v-shape.

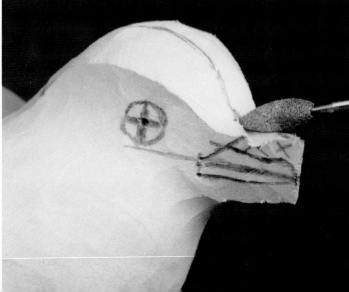

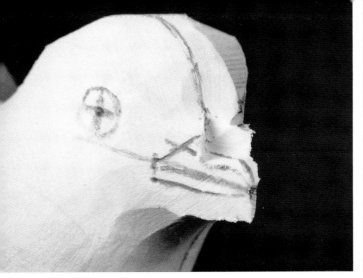

Figure 44. Keep cutting away the excess until you get down to the top mandible line, maintaining a flat plane. Be careful not to undercut the shelf at base of the beak. Redraw the top centerline.

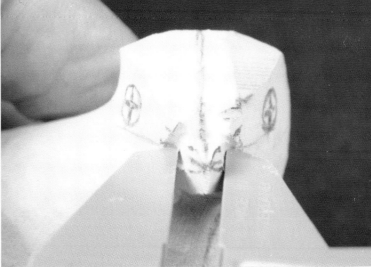

Figure 47. Keep cutting away wood until the width of the base of the beak measures 0.22 inches.

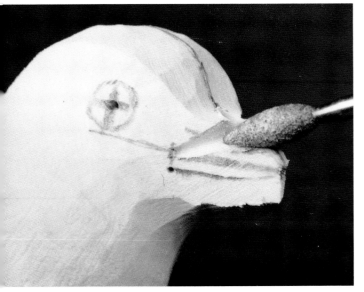

Figure 45. At the side base of the upper mandible, remove a small amount of wood to angle the base toward the commissure line.

Figure 46. Begin removing wood at the sides of the lower mandible. Be sure to keep the side base of the beak straight up and down and to keep equal amounts of wood on each side of the centerline to maintain the beak's balance.

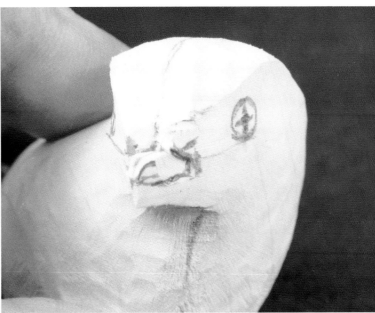

Figure 48. Draw lines at the base of the beak with a sharp pencil point.

Figure 49. Beginning just in front of the eye, flow the sides of the head down to the base of the beak, eliminating the shelf on each side. Then, flow the forehead down to the base of the upper mandible, eliminating that shelf. Do not round the head yet. You will not be carving on the corners of the forehead, but on the flat plane.

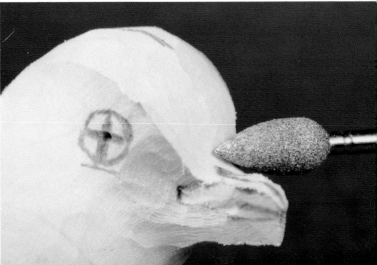

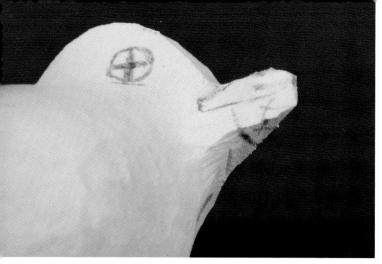

Figure 50. Measure and mark 0.25 inches from the end of the beak on its underside.

Figure 51. Cut away the excess wood underneath the beak back to the measurement line. Keep the bottom of the lower mandible flat.

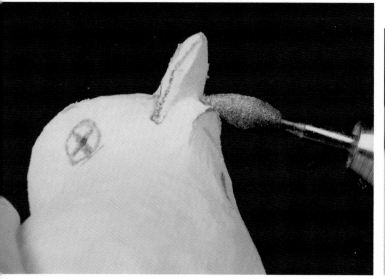

Figure 52. Round the shape of the little tuft of feathers from side to side.

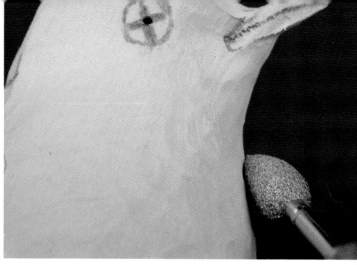

Figure 53. Flow the chin down to the base of lower mandible, eliminating the shelf. Scoop a little wood out of the chin and throat, and round them, blending into the surrounding area.

Figure 54. With a straight-sided stone, smooth and shape the planview of the beak. The beak's width should be 0.11 inches about half-way of its length. Recheck all beak measurements and adjust if necessary.

Figure 55. Redraw the slightly curved commissure lines, making sure that they are equal from the head-on view.

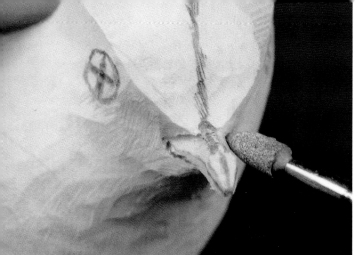

Figure 56. Remove small amounts of wood on each side of the upper mandible, making the culmen narrow just behind the bulbous tip. A stone is useful for this step, since a diamond bit or ruby carver would probably be too aggressive unless you use a very delicate touch.

Figure 57. Round over the bulbous tip on the upper mandible. Round over the sharp corners on the bottom of the lower mandible. Lightly sand the entire beak, eliminating any irregularities. Redraw the commissure lines and draw in balanced nostril placements.

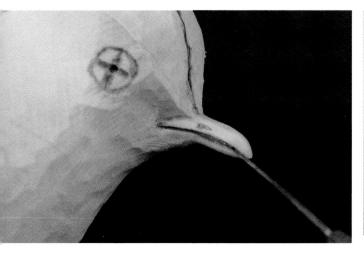

Figure 58. Burn the first stroke on the commissure lines with the pen held perpendicular to the side of the beak.

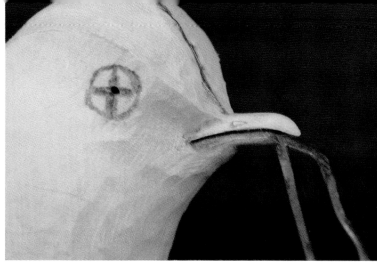

Figure 59. For the second stroke, lay the burning pen down on its side and burn up to the first line. This depresses the side of the lower mandible, and gives the effect of it fitting up and into the upper mandible.

Figure 60. With very low heat on the burning pen, use just the point to burn a short line for the nostril hole on each side. Though on the real bird, the nostril is open from side to side, you do not need to risk damaging the carving by burning completely through.

Figure 61. Lightly sand the entire beak with 400 grit sandpaper. Lightly blow or brush any dust off and saturate the beak with thin super-glue. When dry, fine sand again.

**Killdeer Chick 133**

Figure 62. On the crown above the eyes, measure and mark the head width (0.6 inches). Draw the planview shape of the head encompassing the marks. Note the wedge shape.

Figure 65. Recheck the eye placements. Drill 5 mm eye holes.

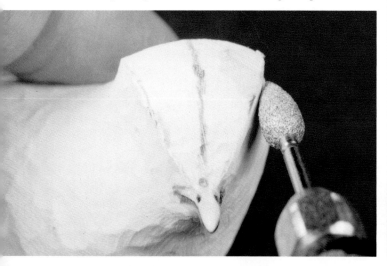

Figure 63. Narrow the crown head width from the eye placements to the top corner. Do not round yet and do not remove any wood from the ear coverts. Keep the sides of the head straight up and down.

Figure 66. Check the eyes for proper fit in the holes.

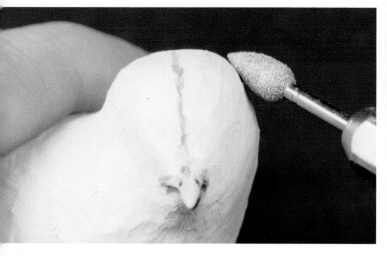

Figure 64. When the head width above the eyes measures 0.6 inches with the calipers, you can round the corners on the head (forehead, crown, and back of head and neck). Flow the hindneck onto the shoulder and mantle areas.

Figure 67. Draw in the ear coverts. They should be of equal length and depth.

Figure 68. Using a small pointed ruby carver, cut around the ear covert. Laying the tool down and using its diameter to cut with will keep it from digging too deeply in the soft wood.

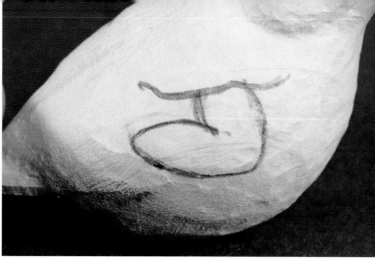

Figure 70. Draw in the winglets and scapular fluffs. The winglets do not have to be balanced on each side. If fact, it will add some motion to the piece if they are not symmetrical.

Figure 69. Flow the channel out onto the surrounding neck area and round over the sharp edge. You may need to remove a small amount of wood from below and in front of the eye to create the needed depression for the eye.

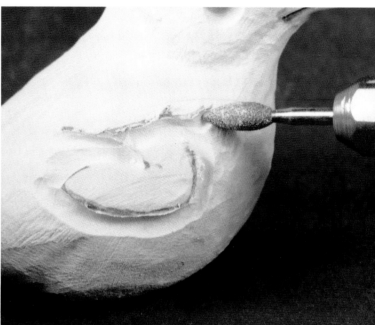

Figure 71. Cut around the winglets and below the scapular fluff line.

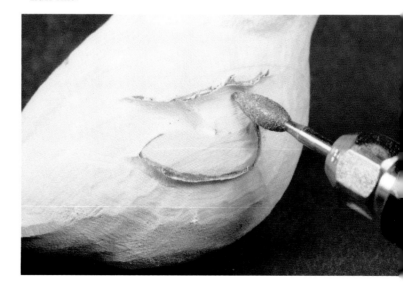

Figure 72. Taper the upper part of the winglet so that it appears as if it is coming out from underneath it. Flow the winglet channels out onto the surrounding flank area.

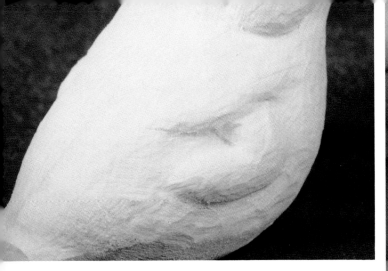

Figure 73. Round over the sharp edges of the winglets and scapular fluffs.

Figure 74. Draw in the lines for the down fluffs. There is no pattern for this. Variety in shape is the goal here.

Figure 75. On the bird's topside, draw in the down fluffs on the hindneck and body.

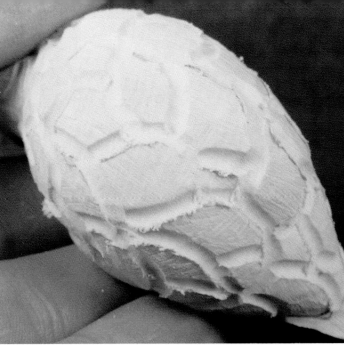

Figure 76. Carve in the channels along the lines. The channels should be slightly deeper on the chick's underside than on the topside.

Figure 77. Round over each of the down fluffs.

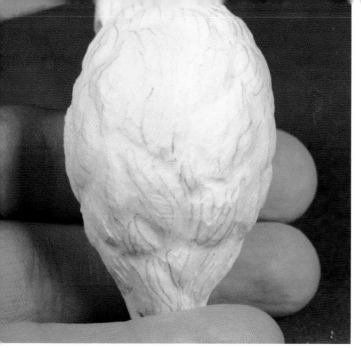

Figure 78. It is helpful to draw in flow lines for the stoning. Vary the directions of the flow to create a pleasing, meandering pattern.

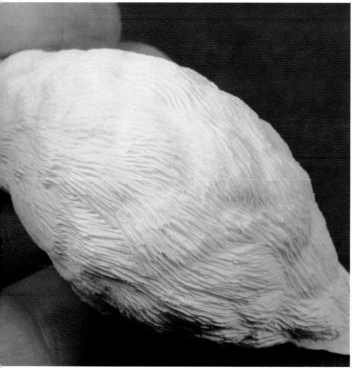

Figure 79. Stone the flow patterns. Using an adjustable light shooting across the surface at a low angle enables you to see the stoning more easily.

Figure 80. Note that the stoning flows to the back of the ear coverts on the side of the head and then on down the hindneck. Generally, the flow is from the head to the tail. You just do not want it to go in straight lines.

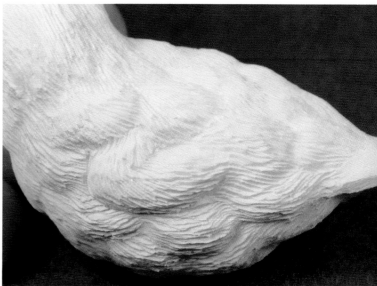

Figure 81. The stoning on the winglet should flow down the forearm (upper winglet part) and then down the hand to the tip.

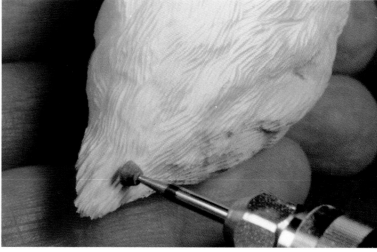

Figure 82. Stone the tail deeply creating different layers of hair-like lines.

Figure 83. Clean the stoning with the laboratory bristle brush on a mandrel.

Figure 84. Begin burning in the down around the beak and work your way back on the chickie. On the head use short strokes with the burning pen tip to simulate the short, bristly downy clumps.

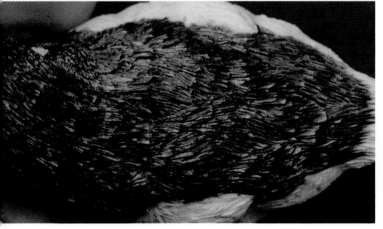

Figure 85. The strokes should be longer when you get back on the body. By burning from front to back, each stroke will determine the length of the previous one. Let the beginning of the stroke go a little deeper and pull up and out on the end of the stroke. This type of indent burning helps to create a layered look.

**138   Killdeer Chick**

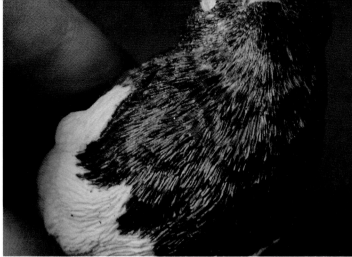

Figure 86. On the underside, start under the chin and burn back toward the tail with short strokes near the head and gradually longer strokes back on the body.

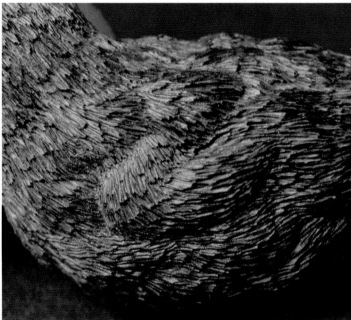

Figure 87. On the winglets, the strokes are not as long as the ones on the body.

Figure 88. The burning is deeper on the tail.

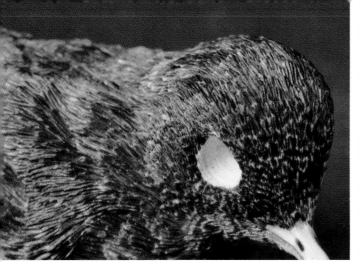

Figure 89. Note the little clumps of down that the indent burning created on the forehead. Clean all of the burning with a toothbrush to remove any carbon deposits.

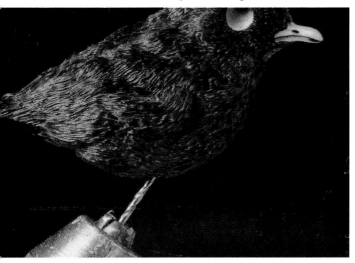

Figure 90. There is no measurement for the exit points of the legs and feet. Since the feet moves in all directions, their position depends on the position of the bird and whatever it is standing on. Unless a bird is in some animated, motion pose, the body should be ballanced over its toes.

Drill 1/16" holes approximately one-half inch deep into the body at the appropriate exit points for the legs and feet. Drilling at the same angle as the leg bone actually goes into a real bird's body helps me to keep the anatomy straight in my mind.

Figure 91. Insert a piece of 16 gauge galvanized wire. For the leg with flat toes, measure and mark 0.3 inches for the bottom of the leg (tibiotarsus), 0.9 inches for the tarsus, and 0.6 inches to go into the mount.

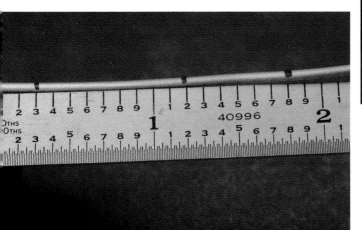

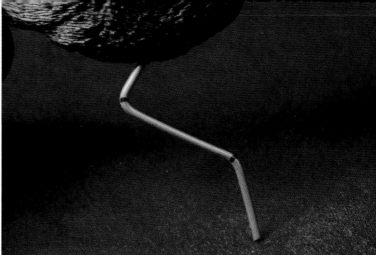

Figure 92. Pull the wire out of the body, cut it off, make the appropriate bends for the mount, and fit it into the body.

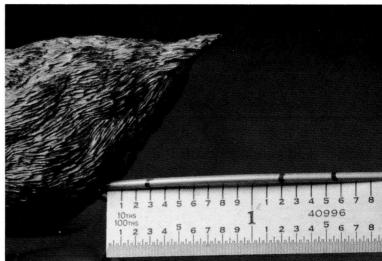

Figure 93. For the bent-toed foot, measure and mark 0.3 inches for the bottom of the leg (tibiotarsus), 0.9 inches for the tarsus, 0.35 inches for the base joint of the middle toe, and 0.6 inches to go into the mount.

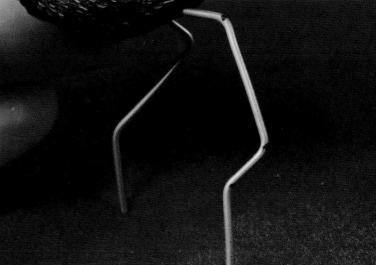

Figure 94. Remove the wire from the body, cut it off, make the appropriate bends, and fit it into the body. Note the extra little bend of the piece for the base middle toe joint.

Figure 95. With both legs in the chick, hold it over the mount and mark where the wires will go. You will likely have to adjust the bends to ensure that the bird is balanced over its toes.

Figure 96. Drill 5/64" diameter holes into the mount and fit the bird in place. You may have to adjust the bends again to get him positioned properly.

Figure 97. Check the bird's position from all angles.

Figure 98. For the flat toes, measure 0.6 inches for the inner toe on a piece of 16 gauge copper wire, bend the wire, measure 0.65 inches for the outer toe, and cut it off. Cut another piece of wire 0.85 inches for the middle toe. With small needle-nose pliers, make the appropriate bends for each claw.

Flatten each claw by placing it on an anvil and tapping it with a hammer. Use a carbide bit to do the final shaping on the claw. Use a piece of sandpaper to remove any burrs created.

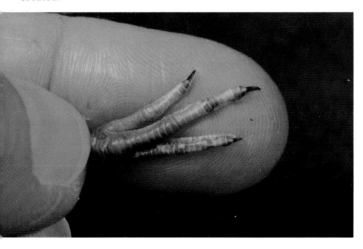

Figure 99. Note the scale markings on the killdeer chick's toes.

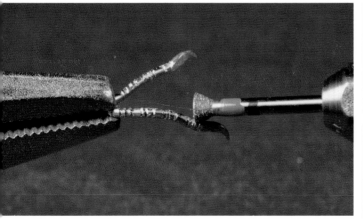

Figure 100. Use a square-edged carbide bit, file, or diamond bit to score the scales on each toe. Remove any roughness with sandpaper.

Figure 101. Fit the toes to the contour of the mount.

Figure 102. For the bent toes, make the inner/outer toe combination as you did for the flat toes. Since the middle toe base joint (0.35 inches long) is part of the foot wire, you will only need a piece 0.5 inches long for the remainder. Create and shape the claws on these toes, and do the scale markings. Do the scale markings on the middle toe base joint (on the foot wire). Bend the toes to fit the mount.

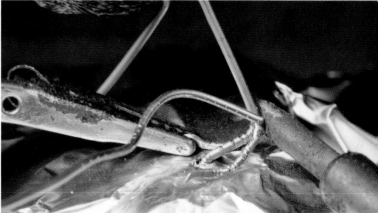

Figure 103. I put a piece of aluminum foil over the pile of rocks to keep them clean. Hold the inner/outer combination in place with a helping hands jig, apply flux, and then solder.

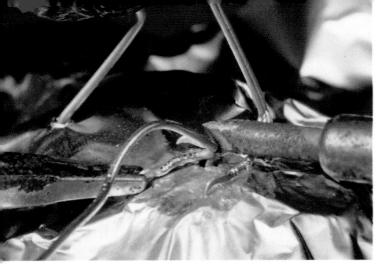

Figure 104. Making sure that there is a straight line from the base of the middle toe to its tip, hold in place, flux, and solder quickly. If you hold the heat on this joint for too long, you may heat and melt the previous joint. You can use a heat sink to absorb some of the heat, but it is just as easy to solder quickly. Flux, touch it with the soldering pen and solder, and get off quick! Wipe off any flux deposits.

Figure 105. Hold the flat toes in place, flux and solder them. Clean any excess flux off the wires.

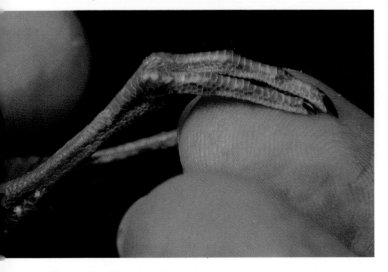

Figure 106. The side view of a killdeer chick's foot and toes.

Figure 107. Note the detail of the ankle and fine reticulated scales on the tarsus and hind tendon.

Figure 108. The back of the tarsus and hind tendon also have the reticulated scales.

Figure 109. To create the pads under the toes, mix up a small amount of the epoxy putty, and roll a fine worm about the diameter of the wire. Heat the toes with a hair dryer, and press a piece of the worm on each toe. Anytime the putty starts sticking to the tool, just plunge it into oily clay. The coat of oil that is left prevents the putty from adhering to the tool. Work on one toe at a time until you have done all three. Press the fine detailing in the sides and bottom of the pads.

Figure 110. The pads should be only slightly wider than the wire toes when they are pressed into position. Put a small flat piece of putty between the outer and middle toes at their base to form a small, short web. Press in texture to resemble wrinkles.

Figure 111. Fit the foot into the mount to make sure that pads conform to the shape.

Figure 112. Heat the tarsus wire with the hair dryer, and start applying the putty for the tibiotarsus, ankle joint, tarsus, hind tendon, and main toe joint covering.

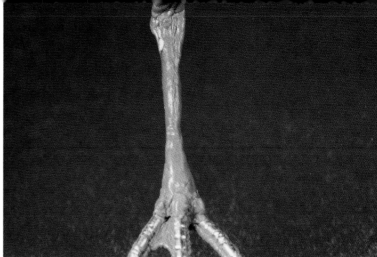

Figure 113. Keep manipulating the putty until the shape and thickness is correct.

Figure 114. Use an empty 0.5 mm mechanical pencil point opening to press in the reticulated scales and details.

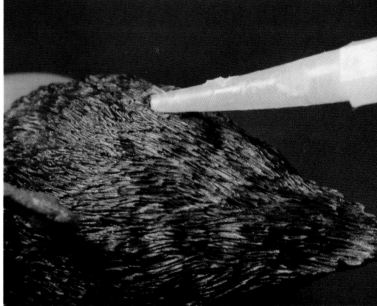

Figure 115. When the putty has hardened, glue one leg at a time, putting the bird in place on the mount each time to make sure it is positioned properly before the glue dries.

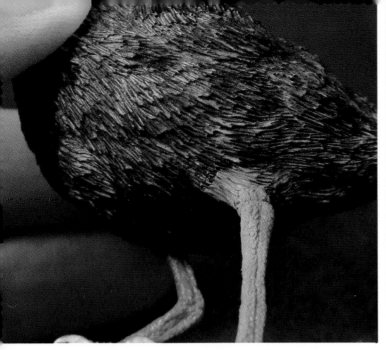

Figure 116. When the glue has dried, mix up a small amount of the epoxy putty, apply a small amount around the tibiotarsus/body joint. Press in the hair-like texture, and blend the putty into the belly texturing.

Figure 118. Spray the entire chick (feet and legs included) with Krylon Crystal Clear 1301.

Figure 117. Set the eyes according to the directions in the Bluebird Chapter. Allow the putty to harden.

Figure 119. Apply several coats of gesso dry-brushed with a stiff bristle brush to the entire bird. When dry, carefully scrape the eyes.

# PAINTING THE KILLDEER CHICK

Liquitex Acrylics (jar) colors:
White = W
Black = B
Burnt umber = BU
Raw umber = RU
Raw sienna = RS
Payne's grey = PG

* Indicates that a small amount should be added.

Figure 1. Note the dark stripe on the forehead.

Figure 2. The chick's head profile view.

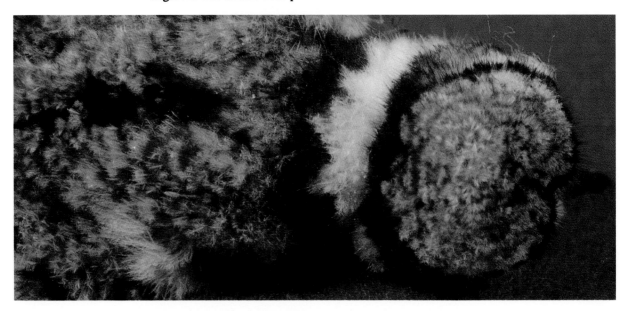

Figure 3. There is an irregular dark stripe down the center of
the back.

Figure 4. The body profile view.

Figure 5. Note the soft greys and charcoal colors on the body.

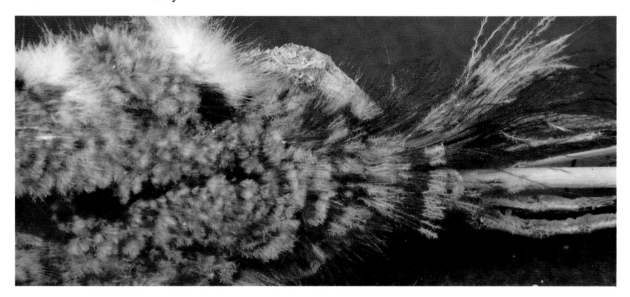

Figure 6. The tail has the barring of the greyish-brown and dark colors.

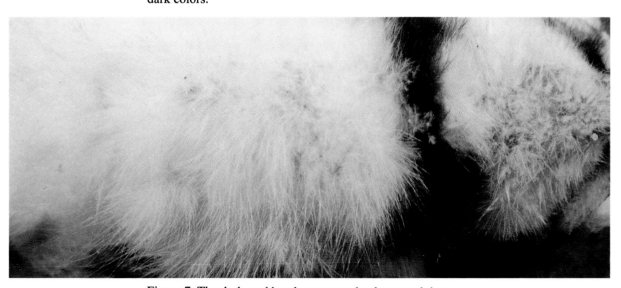

Figure 7. The dark neckband goes completely around the neck. Unlike the mature killdeer with two neckbands, the chick just has a single one.

**Killdeer Chick 147**

Figure 8. Blending burnt umber, black, and a small amount of white to a dark charcoal color, paint in the irregular stripes on the back, tail, winglets, neck, and head.

Fig. 8

BU + B + *W

Figure 10. The dark band should be painted completely around the neck/upper breast.

Figure 9. Carry the dark striping behind and in front of the eye. Give the beak several coats of the dark mixture.

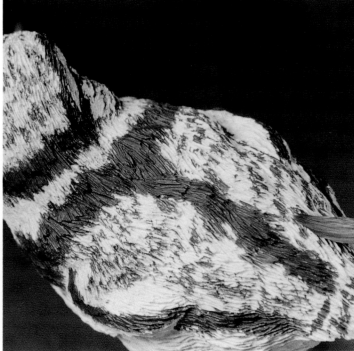

Figure 11. For the irregular spots on the back, lightly dry-brush the dark mixture. Paint the barring on the tail.

Figure 12. Blending white, raw umber, and raw sienna to a beige color, dry-brush in between and occasionally over the spots on the back.

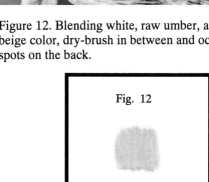

Fig. 12

W + RU + RS

Figure 13. Lightly dry-brush the beige color on the top of the head, ear coverts, middle of the forehead, and above the eyes.

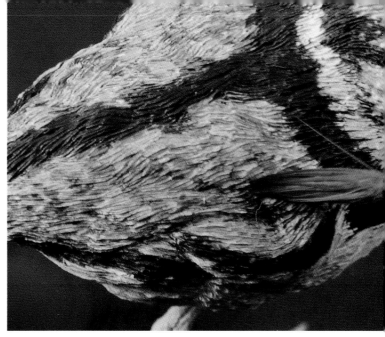

Figure 14. Apply a burnt umber wash on the back, top of winglets, sides of back and rump, and the spaces between the dark barring on the tail.

Fig. 14

BU
Wash

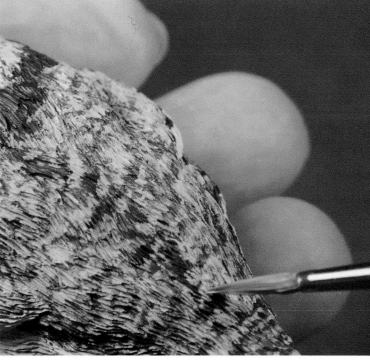

Figure 15. Reapply the dark stripes and spots (BU+B+*W).

**Killdeer Chick 149**

Figure 16. Then, reapply the beige color (W+RU+RS) highlights.

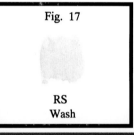

Fig. 17

RS
Wash

Figure 18. Blend more white into the beige mixture and edge the dark stripe with the light mixture, making it more narrow.

Figure 19. It will take as many as 5 or 6 cycles of alternating the lights and darks for the softness to happen. Alternate raw sienna washes with burnt umber washes in between the lights and darks; such as, light, dark, BU wash, light, dark, RS wash, etc.

Figure 17. Apply a thin raw sienna wash.

**150  Killdeer Chick**

Figure 20. Working the lights and darks back and forth several times will create a very soft look to the downy clumps.

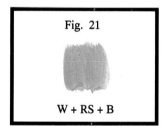

Fig. 21

W + RS + B

Figure 21. Blend white, raw sienna, and black to a light medium grey. Apply several basecoats of this grey to the underside, ear coverts, forehead, stripes above the eyes, hindneck, and winglet ends.

Figure 22. On the forehead, feather the grey into the edges of the dark stripes.

Figure 23. The lighter neckband goes in between the stripe at the base of the hindneck and the lower neckband.

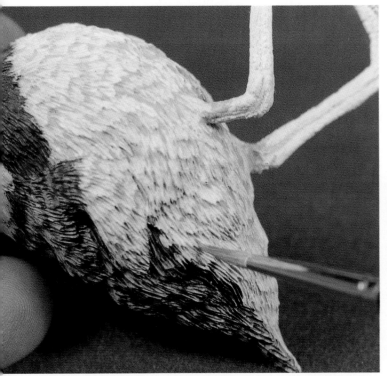

Figure 24. Dry-brush straight white on the edges of the downy clumps on the ear coverts, throat, hindneck band, breast, belly and lower tail coverts. Apply the white highlights several times to reinforce the stark whiteness. When this is dry, apply a very thin white wash.

Figure 25. Blend the dark striping color (BU+B+*W) into the white and the white into the dark color.

Figure 26. Dry-brush a mixture of burnt umber, black, and a small amount of white above the eye and along the edges of all the dark stripes.

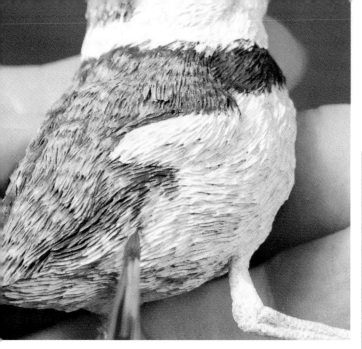

Figure 27. Using straight burnt umber, paint in some medium value barring and irregular spots at the edges of the dark stripes on the flanks.

Figure 28. Lightly dry-brush the burnt umber around the eye.

Figure 29. Apply a wash of a mixture of burnt umber and raw sienna around the eye and on the stripe above the eye.

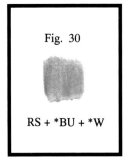

Fig. 30

RS + *BU + *W

Figure 30. Blending raw sienna with small amounts of burnt umber and white, paint the eye rings and lightly around the eyes.

Fig. 31

W + RS + RU

Figure 31. Blend white, raw sienna, and raw umber, and apply several basecoats to the underside of the tail. For the dark striping, mix burnt umber, black, and a small amount of white. Apply a wash with a mixture of white with a small amount of raw umber added.

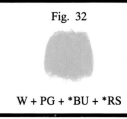

Fig. 32

W + PG + *BU + *RS

Figure 32. For the basecoats on the lower legs, ankles, tarsi, and toes, blend white, payne's grey, burnt umber, and a small amount of raw sienna, and apply several coats.

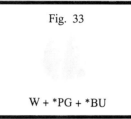

Fig. 33

W + *PG + *BU

Figure 33. Apply a wash with a mixture of white with small amounts of payne's grey and burnt umber.

Figure 34. For the claws, apply a mixture of burnt umber, payne's grey, and a small amount of white.

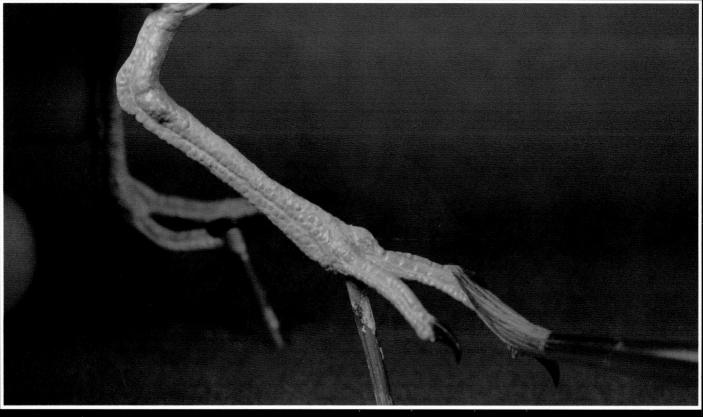

Figure 35. When the claws are dry, mix a small amount of gloss medium in a large puddle of water, and apply to the legs and feet. When this is dry, apply undiluted gloss to the claws.

Figure 36. Apply an equal mixture of matte and gloss mediums to the beak. Scrape the eyes carefully. Glue the chick in place on its mount.

Figure 37. The completed killdeer chick!

# Chapter 6
# Woodie Duckling
## *(Aix sponsa)*

Wood ducks nest near the water in a tree cavity or nest box. The nest is usually nothing more than a lining of white downy feathers unless there is a previous nest of some other creature in the cavity or box. The hen lays 6-15 eggs that are creamy white to beige in color. The hen usually incubates the eggs 28-32 days. The hatchlings have sharp claws that enable them to climb out of the cavity or box at the insistence of their mother's calls. They are not able to fly yet; they just sort of drop to the ground or water. If the nest is above ground, the ducklings are lead to the water by the hen. The young ducks begin to fly at eight to ten weeks old.

The ducklings are born completely covered with down and their eyes open shortly after hatching. The face and underparts are covered with yellowish colored down. There is dark blackish-brown down on the top of the head, back, tail, winglets, and a stripe behind each eye. There are yellowish-white spots on the lower arm edges and the flanks. The bill is dark blackish-brown on the top and brownish-pink at the tip and underneath. The feet are dark blackish- brown with yellowish spots.

## DIMENSION CHART

1. End of tail to wrist: 2.3 inches
2. End of tail to winglet tip: 1.9 inches
3. Length of wing: 1.1 inches
4. Tail length overall: 1.5 inches
5. End of tail to upper tail coverts: 0.2 inches
6. End of tail to lower tail coverts: 0.1 inches
7. End of tail vent: 1.4 inches
8. Head width at ear coverts: 0.9 inches
9. Head width above eyes: 0.55 inches
10. End of bill to back of head: 1.6 inches
11. Bill length
    top: 0.43 inches
    center: 0.55 inches
    bottom center: 0.4 inches
    bottom outer: 0.55 inches
12. End of bill to front of nostril: 0.3 inches
13. Bill height at base: 0.27 inches
14. End of bill to eye center: 0.9 inches, 5 mm brown eyes
15. Bill width at base: 0.21 inches at top; 0.27 inches at commissure
16. Tarsus length: 0.7 inches
17. Tarsus thickness (at narrowest part)
    front to back: 0.13 inches
    side to side: 0.1 inches
18. Toe lengths
    inner: 0.65 inches
    middle: 0.85 inches
    outer: 0.75 inches
    hind: 0.3 inches
19. Body width without wings: 1.6 inches
20. Body length from breast to end of tail: 3.2 inches

## TOOLS AND MATERIALS

Bandsaw (or coping saw)
Flexible shaft machine
Carbide bits
Ruby carvers and/or diamond bits
Variety of mounted stones
Pointed clay tool or dissecting needle
Compass (the kind used to draw circles)
Ruler measuring in tenths of an inch
Calipers measuring in tenths of an inch
Rheostat burning machine
Awl
400 Grit sandpaper
Drill and drill bits
Small cartridge roll sander on a mandrel
Laboratory bristle brush on a mandrel
Needle-nose pliers and wire cutters
Toothbrush
Safety glasses and dustmask
Super-glue and 5 minute epoxy
Oily clay (brand names Plasticene or Plastilena)
Duro ribbon epoxy putty (blue and yellow variety)
Krylon Crystal Clear 1301 Spray
Pair of 5 mm. brown eyes
Tupelo block
    body: 2.0" (H) x 2.2" (W) x 3.2" (L)
    head: 1.3" (H) x 1.0" (W) x 1.7" (L)
    feet: scrap piece
1/4" Hardwood dowel, 4" long
16 Gauge galvanized wire
18 Gauge tempered wire (also known as piano or music wire)
20 Gauge copper wire
0.5 mm mechanical pencil with lead removed

# CARVING THE WOODIE DUCKLING

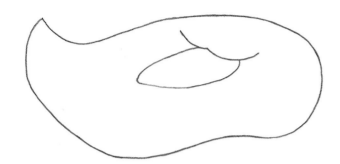

Baby Profile Pattern

Head Profile Pattern

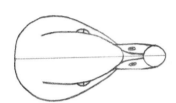

Top Plainview of Head

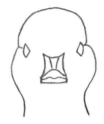

Head-on View

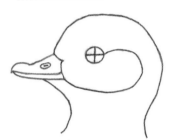

Profile View of Head

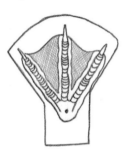

Toe Block Pattern
( Left Foot Drawn )

Foot

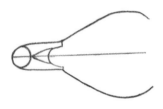

Detail of Underside
of Lower Mandible

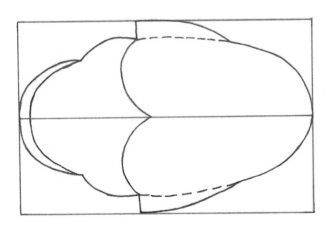

Under Plainview *

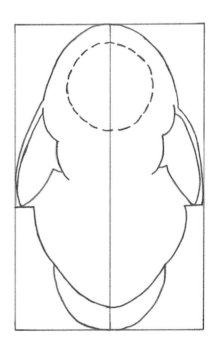

Top Plainview *

\* Foreshortening may cause distortions on plainviews.
  Check the dimension chart.

**160   Woodie Duckling**

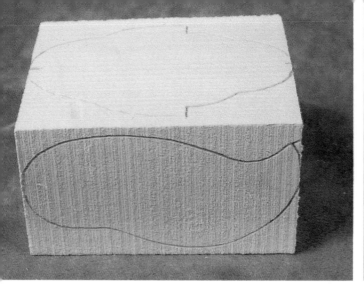

Figure 1. Transfer the profile and planview patterns to the tupelo block, making sure that the front of the breast and the end of the tail match on the respective sides.

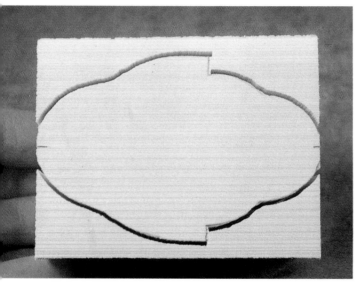

Figure 2. Cut out the planview of the block first, leaving small uncut sections at the back of each winglet.

Figure 3. Next, cut out the profile view completely.

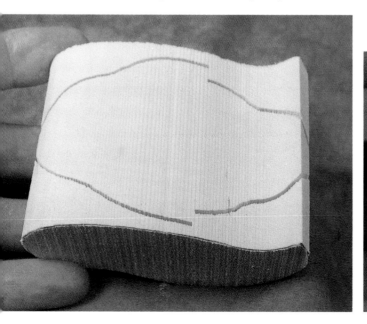

Figure 4. Carefully, cut the small section at the back of each winglet.

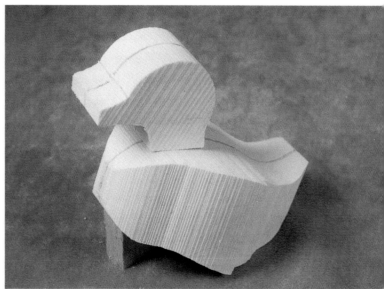

Figure 5. Transfer the profile pattern of the head to the other smaller tupelo block, and cut out the profile. Draw in centerlines on both the head and body blocks.

Figure 6. Draw diagonal lines from corner to corner on the bottom of the head block, marking the center where the lines cross.

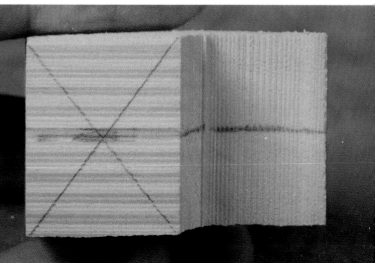

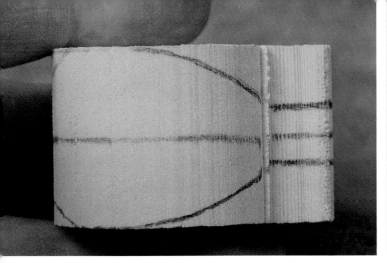

Figure 7. Transfer the planview pattern to the head blank.

Figure 8. Bandsaw or carve away the excess outside of the lines, keeping the sides of the head and bill straight up and down.

Figure 9. Using the profile pattern, transfer the bill drawings to the blank. Use a ruler or calipers to check all dimensions. On the top centerline, measure and mark the top bill length (0.43 inches).

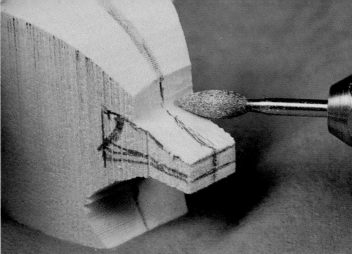

Figure 10. With a medium pointed ruby carver, grind away the excess wood above the bill and back to the top bill length measurement mark, keeping it flat at this time. Redraw the centerline.

Figure 11. The top planview of the duckling's bill.

Figure 12. Carefully, draw in the top planview bill shape out on the tip.

Figure 13. Cut away the excess from around the tip planview, keeping the sides straight up and down.

Figure 14. The profile view of the duckling's bill.

Figure 15. Note that the bottom of the bill is wider than the top of the bill.

Figure 16. Redraw any lines cut away. Slowly and carefully, begin cutting away the waste wood from the sides of the bill, leaving it wider at the bottom than at the top.

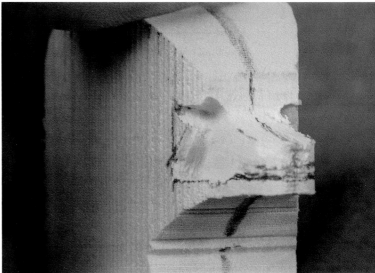

Figure 17. Grind off a little from one side, then some from the other side, and then check from the head-on view to make sure the bill is balanced across the centerline.

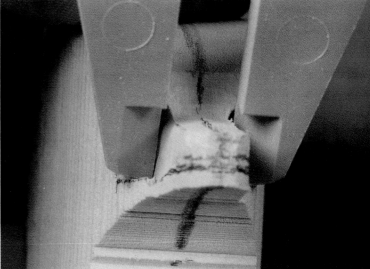

Figure 18. Keep removing the excess until the bottom of bill measures 0.27 inches from side to side.

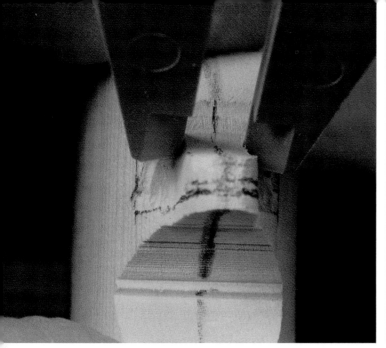

Figure 19. Across the top of bill should measure 0.21 inches.

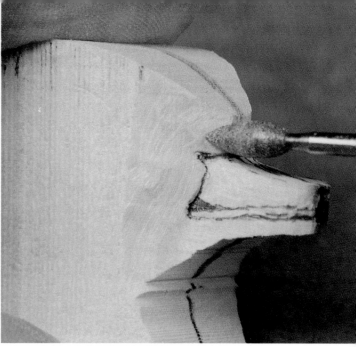

Figure 21. Flow the sides of the head down to the base of the bill and eliminate the shelf.

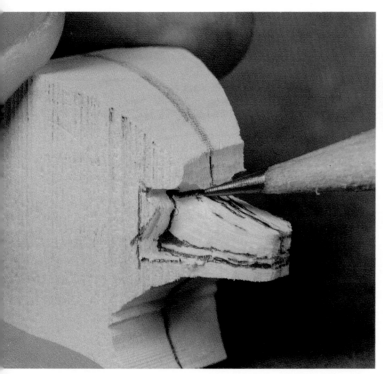

Figure 20. With the point of a sharpened pencil, trace around the inside perimeter of the base of the beak. Redraw the bottom edge of the upper mandible.

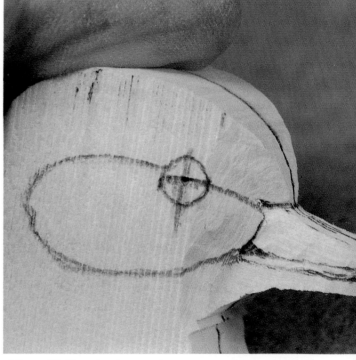

Figure 22. Transfer the eye placements to sides of the head. Check with ruler to see that the center of each is 0.9 inches from the end of the bill. Pinprick the eye centers deeply. Draw a line from the top of the bill through the eye and loop it around the cheek forming the ear covert. Check from the head-on view that the oval shapes are of equal length and depth. Do not let the lower line drop down too low, as it gives a sad, sag-jawed look to the duckling.

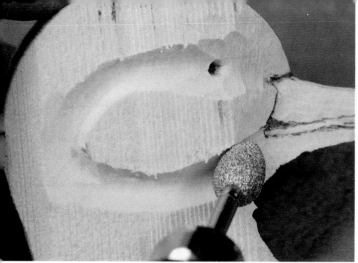

Figure 23. With a medium pointed ruby carver, cut a channel from the top of the bill, through the eye, around the ear covert, and back to the base of the bill.

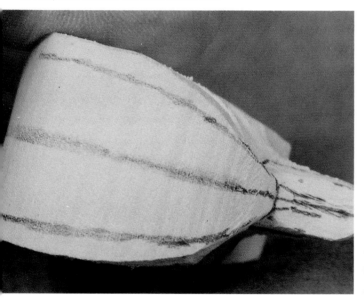

Figure 24. On the top of the head across the crown, measure and mark the head width above the eyes (0.55 inches) across the centerline. Draw in the wedge shape of the head encompassing the measurement marks.

Figure 25. Flow the eye channel up to the top of the head, narrowing the crown width to 0.55 inches above the eyes and up to the other planview lines from the step before. Flow the ear covert channel out onto the surrounding head and neck.

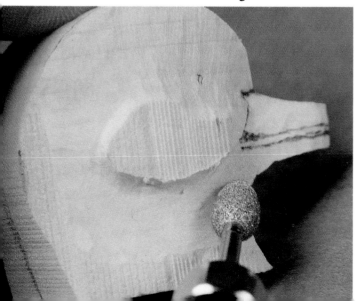

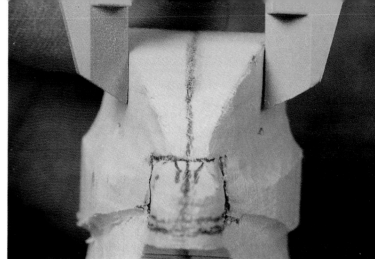

Figure 26. Check the head width above the eyes with the calipers.

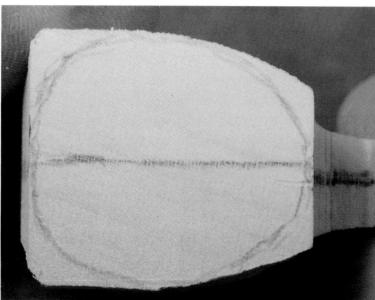

Figure 27. Draw a fat oval on the bottom of the neck.

Figure 28. Round the bottom of the neck and reduce its size to that of the oval.

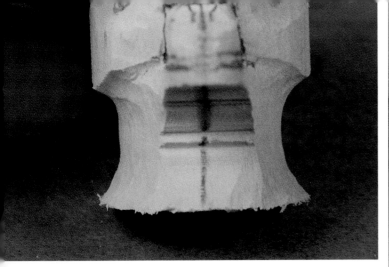

Figure 29. Scoop out the sides of the neck between the jaw and the bottom of the head blank.

Figure 30. Thin the neck width from side to side to 0.7 inches, keeping equal amounts of wood on each side of the centerline.

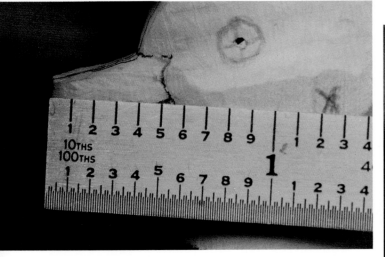

Figure 31. Mark a spot on each ear covert 1.25 inches from the end of the bill. Check from all views to make sure that these marks are equally placed on the cheeks. These are the widest areas on the ear coverts or cheeks. The head width between these two marks should measure 0.9 inches with the calipers. If yours is wider than this, reduce the width to 0.9 inches and remark the high spots again.

Figure 32. Flow the cheeks/ear coverts to the base of the bill, but do not remove any wood from the high spot marks.

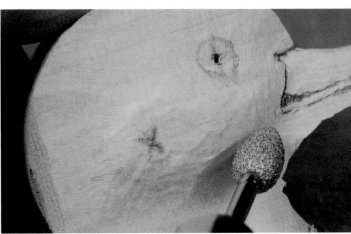

Figure 33. Round over the ear coverts.

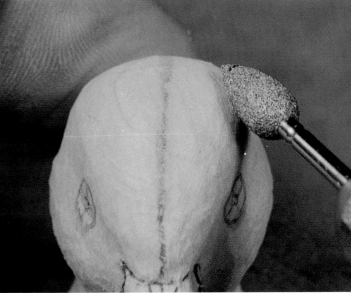

Figure 34. Round over the sharp corners on the forehead, crown, and hindneck.

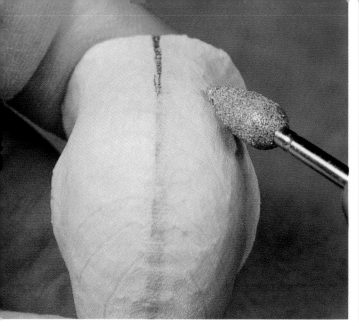

Figure 35. You will need to remove a small amount of wood to ensure that the hindneck profile shape is slightly concave.

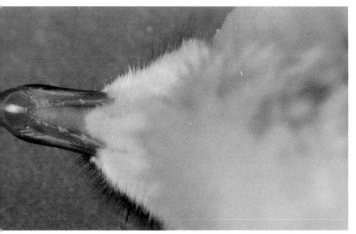

Figure 36. The underside of the duckling's lower mandible.

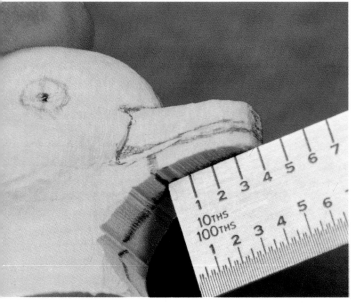

Figure 37. Measure and mark 0.4 inches from the end of the bill on the underside.

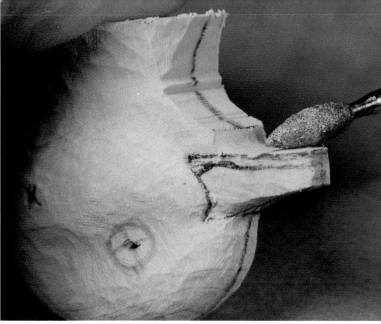

Figure 38. With a medium pointed ruby carver, grind away the excess wood underneath the lower mandible up to the line and back to the measurement line, keeping the surface flat.

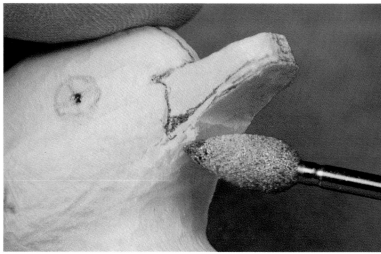

Figure 39. Flow the shelf down from the chin to the bottom of the lower mandible.

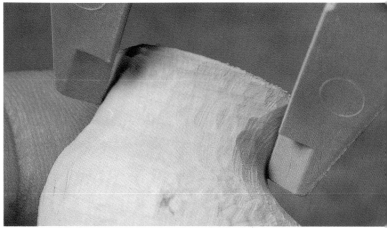

Figure 40. Thin the neck width from front to back to 0.8 inches.

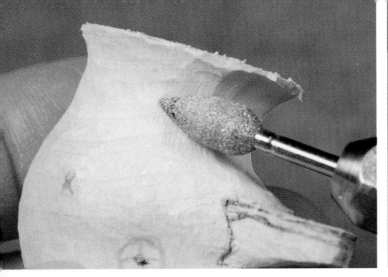

Figure 41. Round the chin and throat and blend into the sides of the neck.

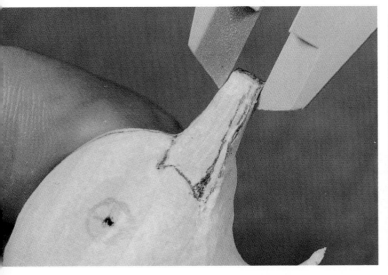

Figure 42. Check the height of the bill tip. It should measure 0.15 inches just back of the tip. If necessary, thin to this dimension.

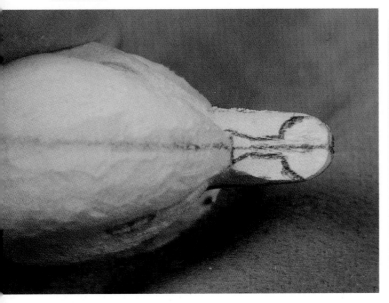

Figure 43. Draw in the key-hole shape on the top of the upper mandible.

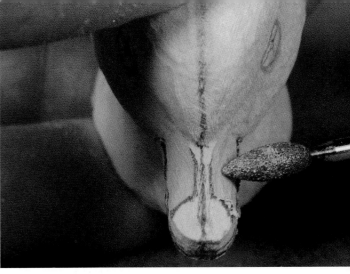

Figure 44. Angle the sides of the upper mandible from the base of the bill out to the nail oval and from the commissure line to the culmen line. Leave the culmen and nail oval flat.

Figure 45. Round over the nail oval, leaving it a bulbous tip. Transfer the nostrils from the profile and planview patterns, making sure that they are balanced on each side of the centerline.

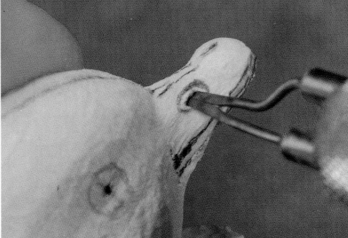

Figure 46. With a very small pointed burning pen, burn the slits in the nostrils, holding the pen horizontal. Though on a real bird, the nostrils go all the way through, it is not really necessary to do this in the carving.

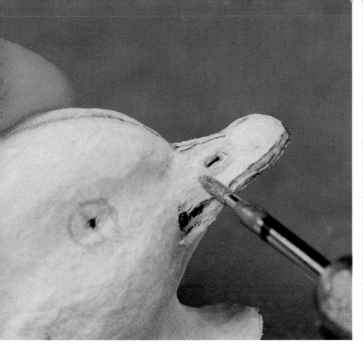

Figure 47. Using a very small blunt pointed diamond bit, carve around the nostril pads, and flow out onto the surrounding bill. Round over the edges of the pads. Smooth the nostril pads and the entire upper mandible with a stone.

Figure 49. To make sure that the corner of a stone is sharp-edged, run it at medium speed and hold it lightly to a dressing stone. Always wear safety glasses or goggles when carving; eyes are too precious to lose! But especially safeguard your eyes when using a dressing stone. The little bits of excess stone come flying off that little bugger at breakneck speed, and it would only take one speck to cause an eye irreparable harm!

Figure 48. Burn in the detail line just above the bottom edge of the upper mandible on each side.

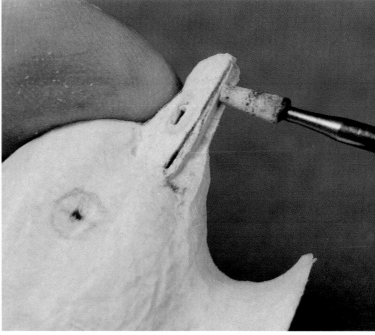

Figure 50. Using the sharp-edged stone, relieve underneath the side edges of the upper mandible, leaving a small shelf overhang (about 1/32").

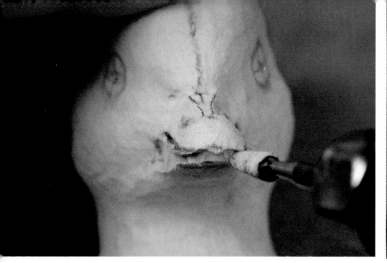

Figure 51. There is a double "s"-curve at the tip of the upper mandible. Use the sharp-edged stone to carve in the wavy overhang.

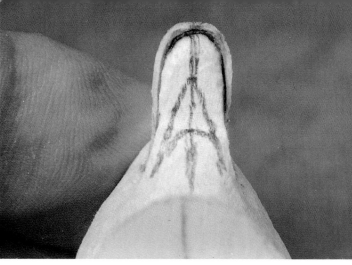

Figure 54. Draw in the details on the underside of the lower mandible, the v-shape and u-shape.

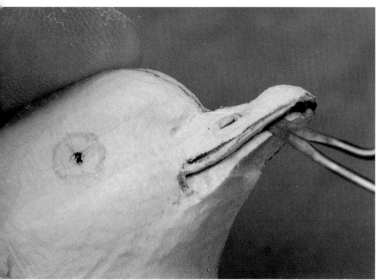

Figure 52. Use a burning pen to lightly burn tight in the corner of the overhang. Be careful that you do not use so much heat or press so hard that you come through the upper mandible. Use a light touch and low heat.

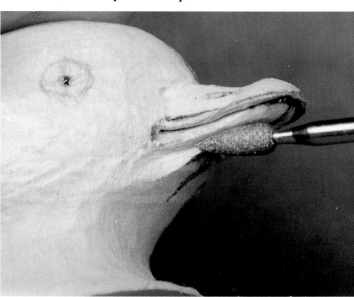

Figure 55. Using a small ruby carver, cut around the u-shaped tuft of feathers on the chin, creating a shelf and keeping the bottom of the lower mandible flat at its base. The bottom of the lower mandible should go straight into the head and not curve up toward the eye.

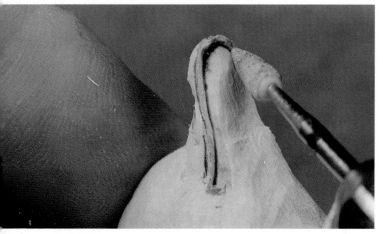

Figure 53. At the tip of the bill underneath, use a small pointed stone to round the end up to the burn line, so that the lower mandible tucks up into the bottom of the upper mandible.

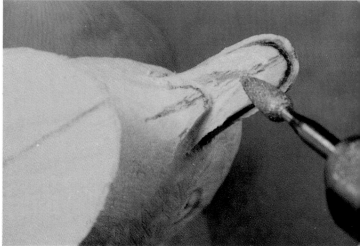

Figure 56. Cut the v-shape into the lower mandible's surface.

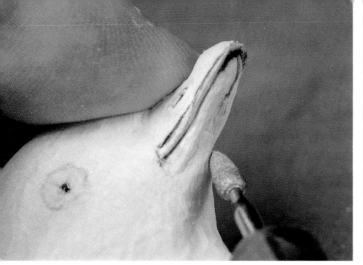

Figure 57. Round over the little u-shaped tuft of feathers on the chin and flow them down to the base of the lower mandible.

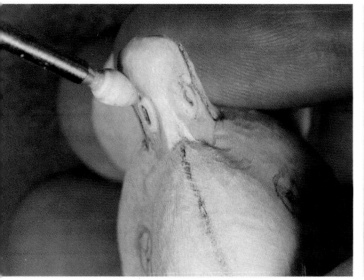

Figure 58. Generally smooth the entire bill with a stone or fine sandpaper, lightly rounding over all sharp corners.

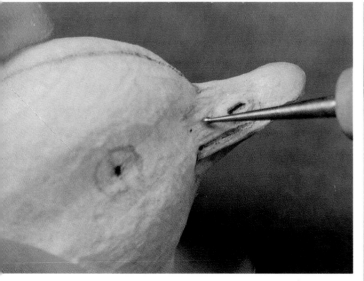

Figure 59. Press in a few wrinkles along the base of the upper mandible using a stylus or the dull point of a hard pencil.

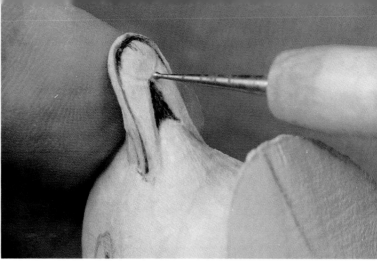

Figure 60. Press in an oval shape on the tip of the underside of the lower mandible. Using a small pointed burning pen, burn in the wrinkly texturing in the v-shaped depression.

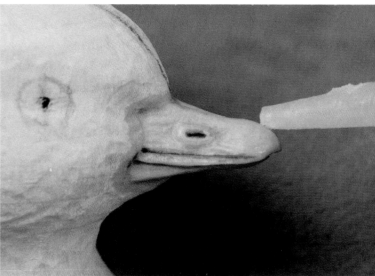

Figure 61. Saturate the bill with thin super-glue. When this is dry, fine sand with 400 grit paper.

Figure 62. Recheck eye positions and drill 5 mm eye holes balanced on each side of the head.

Figure 63. Check the eyes for proper fit.

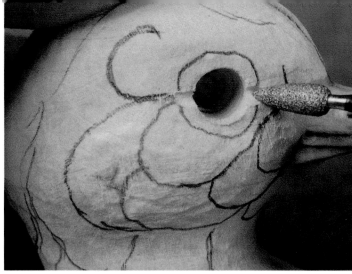

Figure 66. Using the smallest pointed ruby carver, cut in the front and rear corners of the eyes.

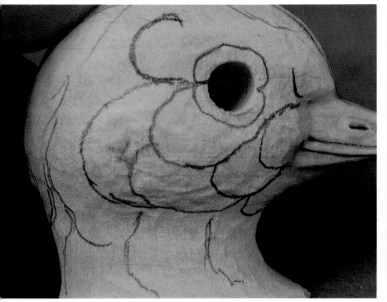

Figure 64. Draw in the contouring on the head.

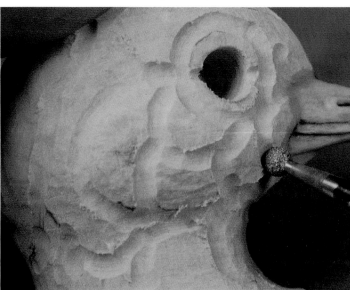

Figure 67. Channel all of the contouring lines using a small ruby carver or diamond ball.

Figure 65. Note that all of the lines flow to the back of the head, but there are no straight lines.

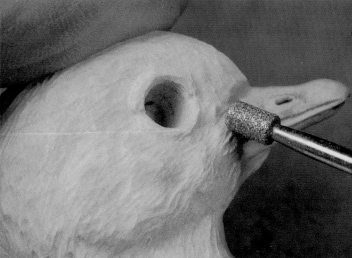

Figure 68. To facilitate the variations in fluff heights, carve furrows in the down fluffs on the head except for the small ones around the eyes.

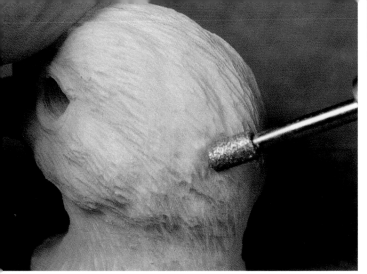

Figure 69. The furrows should flow to the back of the head and down the neck.

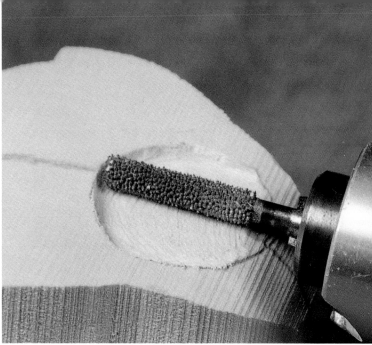

Figure 72. Flatten the area where the base of the neck will sit.

Figure 70. Fit the head on the body.

Figure 73. Fit the neck down into body.

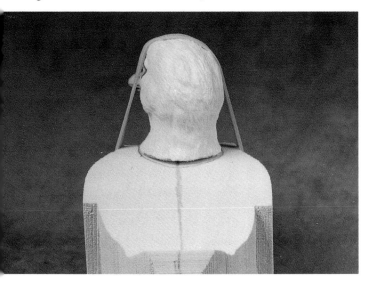

Figure 71. The center of the neck should be balanced over the center of the body. Mark the placement around the neck edges with a pencil.

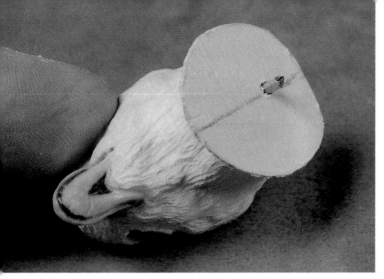

Figure 74. Drill a 1/16" diameter hole one-quarter inch deep into the neck. Fit a piece of 16 gauge galvanized wire into the neck leaving about 1/8" protruding.

Figure 77. Note the shape of the duckling's winglet.

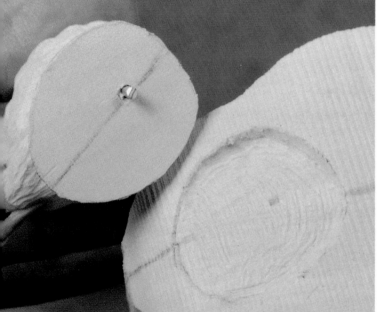

Figure 75. Hold the head in place over the body and press lightly to leave a dent mark on the body. Drill 1/16" diameter hole one-quarter inch deep at the dent mark. Replace the short wire in the neck with a slightly longer one.

Figure 76. Fit the head to the body and mark placement lines several places around the neck's circumference.

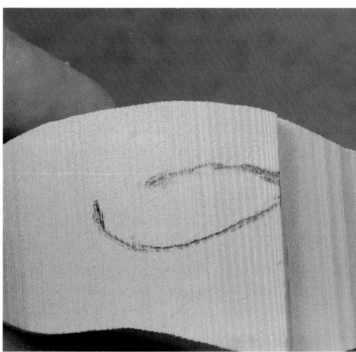

Figure 78. Draw in the winglets on the carving.

Figure 79. Different winglet positions add to the animation and motion of the carving.

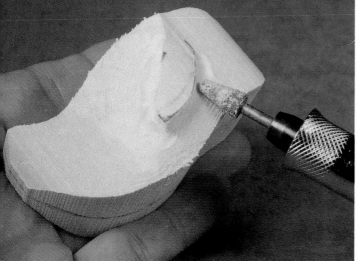

Figure 80. Cut around each of the winglets down to the flanks.

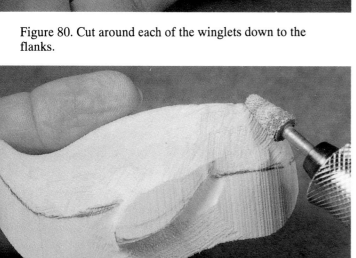

Figure 81. Draw in a centerline on the sides of the body. Round the top part of the body from the top centerline to each of the side centerlines.

Figure 82. Note the placement marks around the neck joint. Putting a small amount of super-glue down in the body hole and allowing the glue to harden the wood will keep the hole from getting sloppy. Do not glue the head in place at this time.

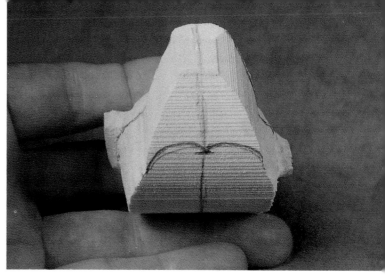

Figure 83. Measure and mark the vent 1.4 inches from the end of the tail. Draw in the baby-bottom shape.

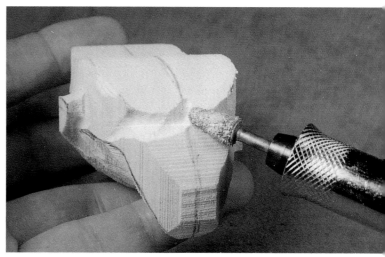

Figure 84. Channel around the vent lines (deeper on the blank's corners) and up to the side centerlines. The channel on the flanks should be at an angle pointing towards the head and should gradually end at the side centerline.

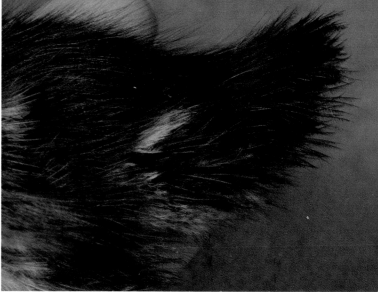

Figure 85. The woodie duckling's flank and tail.

Figure 86. Round over the lower tail coverts from the vent to the end of the tail and from side to side.

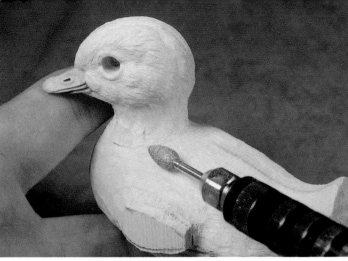

Figure 89. Put the head in place and flow the breast and shoulder area up to the neck.

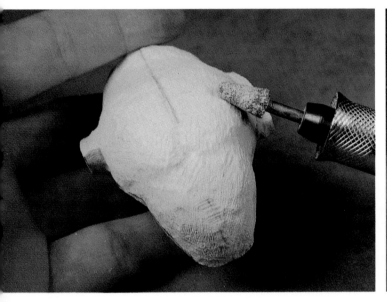

Figure 87. Round over the belly from underneath each winglet to the centerline. Flow the vent ledges down to the base of the lower tail coverts.

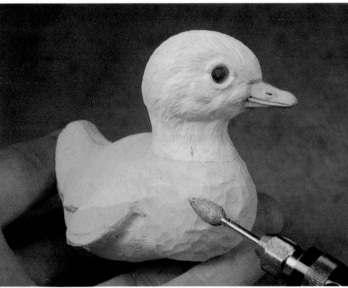

Figure 90. Reduce the size of the ball of the breast so that the little chickie is not too breasty.

Figure 88. Round over the breast area.

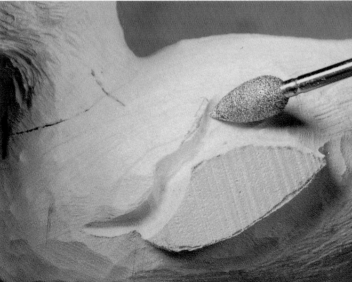

Figure 91. Draw in the upper winglet/scapular fluffs above each winglet. Channel underneath each fluff.

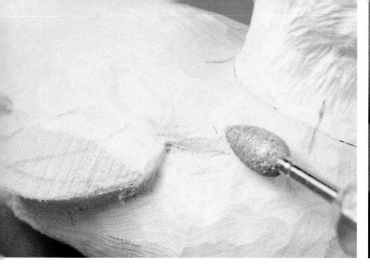

Figure 92. Flow the channel out onto the winglet and round over the sharp ledges on the fluffs.

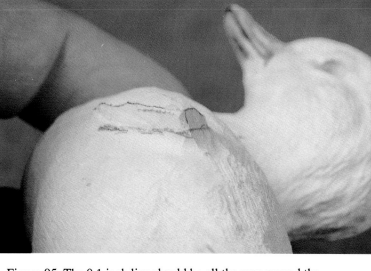

Figure 95. The 0.1 inch line should be all the way around the winglet.

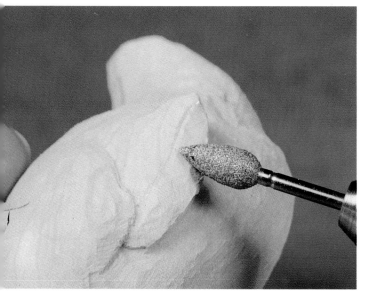

Figure 93. Draw a line down the center of each winglet. Lightly round the surface from the centerline to the winglet's outer edges.

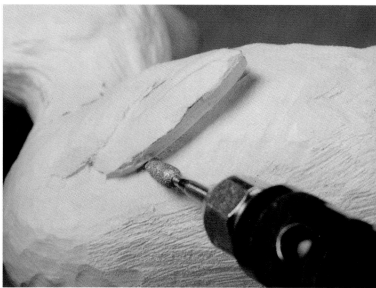

Figure 96. Using the smallest pointed ruby carver, cut away the excess wood under the winglet tips and flow out onto the flank area.

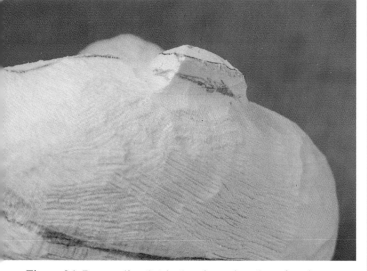

Figure 94. Draw a line 0.1 inches from the edge of each winglet. This allows for the proper thickness of the actual winglet.

Figure 97. Divide the thickness of each winglet by drawing a centerline along each edge.

**Woodie Duckling  177**

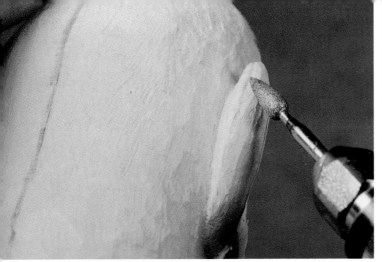

Figure 98. Lightly round over each winglet edge to the centerline on the top and underside.

Figure 101. Use an awl to mark the hole for the drill bit to keep it from drifting.

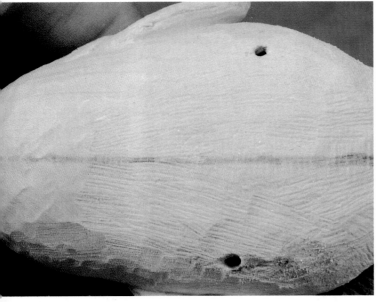

Figure 99. Mark the locations of the feet and legs, approximately 0.6 inches from the centerline. Note that for this particular pose, one foot will be slightly forward of the other.

Figure 100. Trace the toes/web pattern onto a scrap block of tupelo. Cut out with a bandsaw or coping saw. The left set of toes is to be the bent set, so the block for this needs to be 0.5 inches thick. The flat set thickness should be 0.25 inches.

Figure 102. Place the toe blocks on a scrap piece of wood to keep the bottom of the holes from splintering out. Drill 15/64" diameter holes into the back of the blocks going completely through the flat toe block and about three-quarters through the bent toe block.

Figure 103. Super-glue 1/4" hardwood dowels into each toe block. The length of the dowels should be about 2 inches, allowing extra length for a handle.

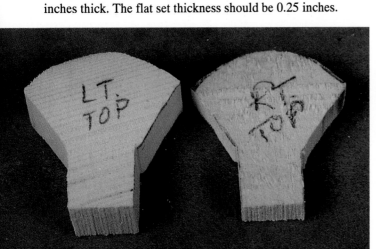

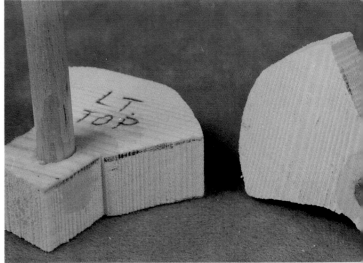

Figure 104. When the glue has hardened, draw the profile view of each set of toes on the sides of their respective blocks.

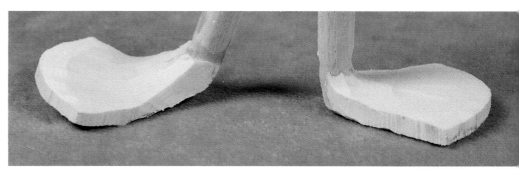

Figure 105. Keeping the tops and bottoms of the toe blocks flat, carve away the excess above and below the lines. Handle the feet gently and do not put excess pressure on any part of them.

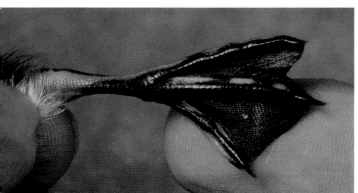

Figure 106. Note the details of the toe joints and webs on the top planview of the duckling's foot.

Figure 107. The hind toe attaches to the tarsus slightly above the main toe joint.

Figure 108. Note the details on the underside of the duckling's foot.

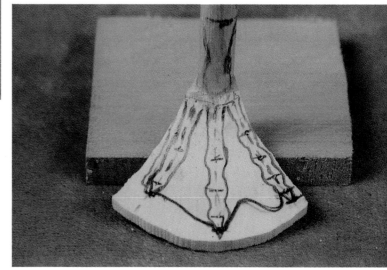

Figure 109. Transfer the toe and tarsus details from the planview pattern.

Figure 110. Shape the tarsus by carving away the excess from its sides. The tarsus width should be 0.1 inches at its narrowest point from side to side.

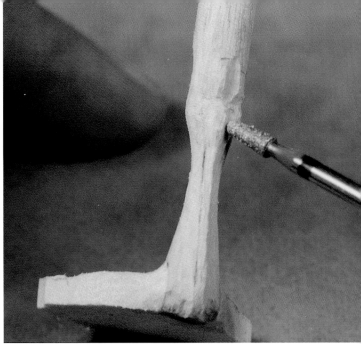

Figure 113. Carve channels on each side of the hind tendon on each foot down the length of the tarsus and on the ankle. Lightly round over all sharp edges. On the front of the tarsus, carve in a small depression at the ankle joint.

Figure 111. Cut away some of the excess from around the toes and webs.

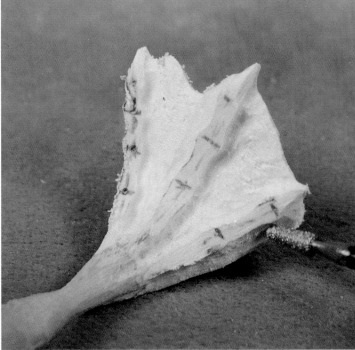

Figure 112. Shape the front and back of the tarsus. The tarsus width from front to back is 1.3 inches. With a small ruby carver or diamond bit, carve the crease at the ankle joint.

Figure 114. With a small blunt-tip diamond bit, lower the webs by cutting around each of the toes, but do not make the webs too thin. Leave the toe joints slightly wider than the toes in between. There is a small flange on the outside of each inner and outer toe. Cut along the outer edge of all the inner and outer toes, but do not carve away this flange. Carve away the excess from each side of the claws and round the top surface of each claw down, but do not undercut yet. Shape the underside of the raised set of toes.

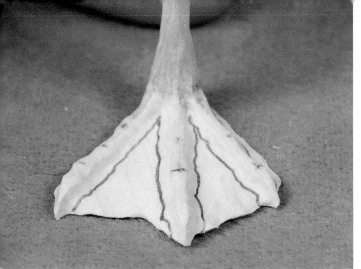

Figure 115. Carve away the excess along the webs' edges. There is a small flange (on both sides of each toe) that is slightly raised from the web. Draw in the flanges keeping the edge irregular. Round over all sharp edges on the toes and feet with stones of appropriate shapes and sizes.

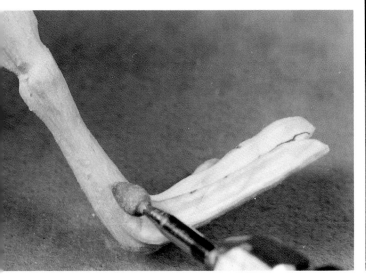

Figure 116. Carve a small channel from the outer flanges to the side of the tarsus on the inner and outer toes.

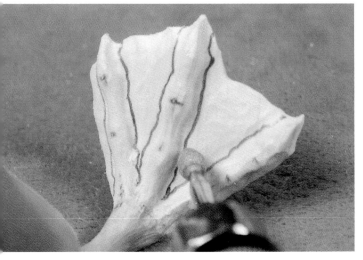

Figure 117. With a small blunt-tip stone, relieve a small amount of wood along the edges of the flanges.

Figure 118. Draw in the scales on the toes and the wrinkle details on the webs and flanges.

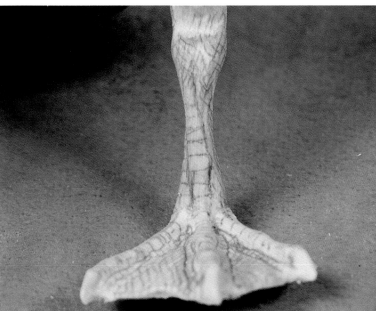

Figure 119. Draw in the scales and wrinkles on the tarsi and ankles.

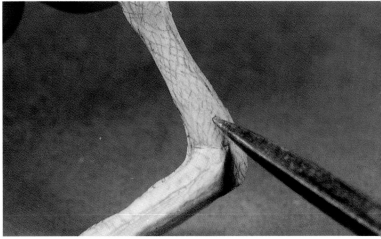

Figure 120. Mark the placement of the hind toe attachment on the inside of each tarsus just above the main toe joint (0.25 inches).

Figure 121. On the bottom of the flat set of toes, make a small hole into the hardwood dowel.

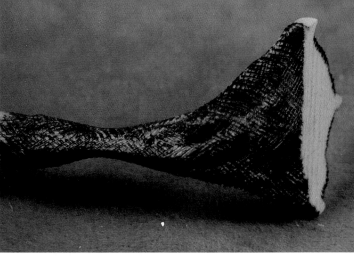

Figure 124. On the bottom of the bent toes, the cross-hatching should be burned up to the flat part.

Figure 122. Burn in the scales and wrinkle detail on the webs, toes, tarsi and ankles. A small pointed burning pen is helpful when working on these delicate feet.

Figure 125. Cut the excess off the dowels just above the ankle joint, and contour the top of the dowel to that of the body.

Figure 126. Cutting the end of a piece of tempered wire with wire cutters will leave a burr that is an excellent substitute for a small wire drill bit. Using a small piece of 18 gauge tempered wire (with a burr on its end), carefully drill into the top of each dowel about 0.3 inches deep. Make sure that the wire goes straight into the body of the dowel and does not angle towards any side.

Figure 123. The extra length of the hardwood dowel provides a handle when working on each foot.

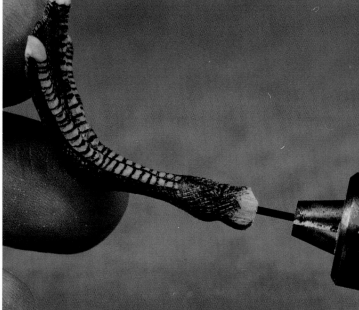

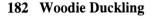

Figure 127. Also drill into bottom of the dowel of the flat foot. Again, be careful to drill into the center of the dowel, sighting it from all angles for straightness.

Figure 128. Smoothing the burr off the end of a piece of the 18 tempered wire will allow it to slip into its drilled hole more easily.

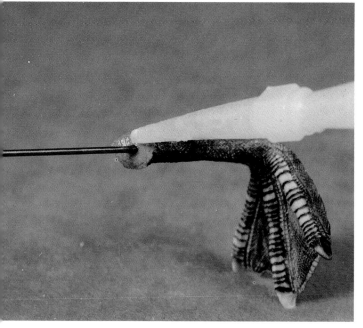

Figure 129. Super-glue a short piece of the tempered wire with its end rounded over into the top of each foot.

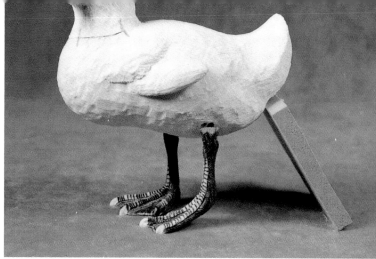

Figure 130. Cut off each wire leaving about 0.6 inches to go into the body. Hold the bird in a natural position, and press the wire of each foot into the body at the placement marks on the underside and at the appropriate angle. The tempered wire slips fairly easily into soft tupelo. Do not glue into body yet.

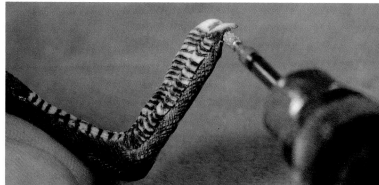

Figure 131. Now, back to finishing up the really fragile parts of the feet. Remove them from the body. With a very small diamond bit, grind away the excess wood from under each claw. Lightly and very carefully sand each claw.

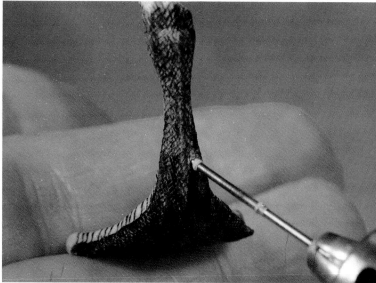

Figure 132. At the hind toe marks on the inside of each tarsus, use the burred piece of 18 gauge tempered wire to drill a shallow hole (about 0.1 inches deep) into the dowel at an angle.

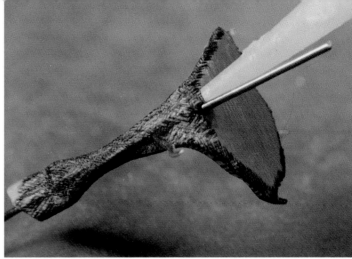

Figure 135. Glue a short piece of 18 gauge tempered wire into the hole on the flat-toed foot and allow to harden.

Figure 133. Cut two pieces of 20 gauge copper wire 0.4 inches long. Shape the curvature of the claw with a small pair of needle-nose pliers on one end of each of the toe wires. Hammer the claws flat on an anvil by tapping them with a hammer. Use a carbide cutter to remove the excess from each claw from the hook. Lightly sand away any burrs. Put a little super-glue on the straight end of the hind toe wire and push into the hole on the inside of the tarsus 0.1 inches deep, leaving a 0.3 inches protruding. Put a little super-glue around the joint to ensure stability.

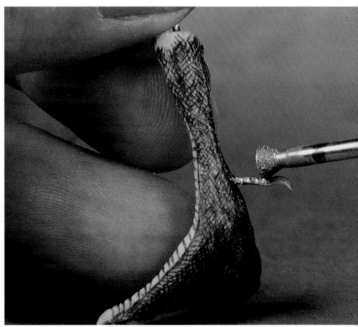

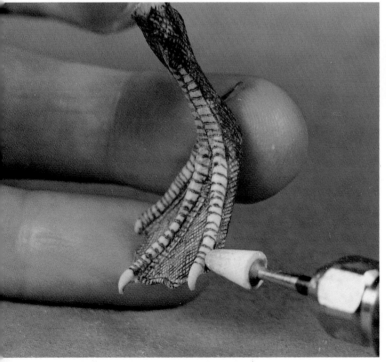

Figure 136. Lightly score the scales on the top of the hind toes with a small inverted-cone diamond bit.

Figure 137. Mix up a small amount of the epoxy putty. Roll a small worm about the diameter of the hind toe wire. Heat the wire with a hair dryer, and press the putty to adhere to the underside of the hind toe. Press in the wrinkly texturing on the pads' sides and underside. Place a small amount around the insertion joint and press in the texturing using an empty 0.5 mm mechanical pencil point. Put the feet aside to rest awhile, until the body is completed.

Figure 134. Lightly go over the burning on the feet and legs with a fine stone or fine sandpaper.

Figure 138. The hair-like downy fluffs on the body of the duckling are small on the front of the body and larger towards the rear.

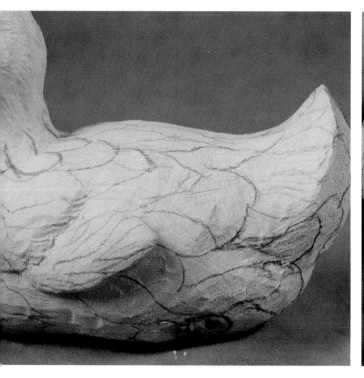

Figure 139. Draw in the variable contouring.

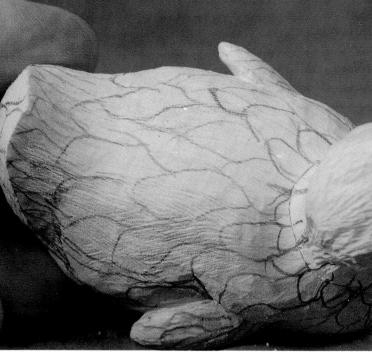

Figure 140. The downy clumps have elongated shapes.

**Woodie Duckling  185**

Figure 141. The clumps on the breast, throat, and neck are more pointed.

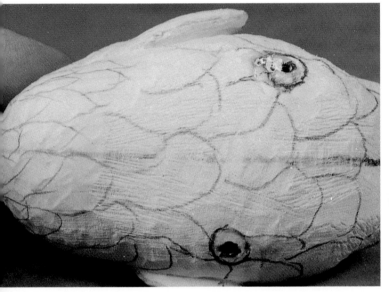

Figure 142. On the belly, the downy clumps are rounded.

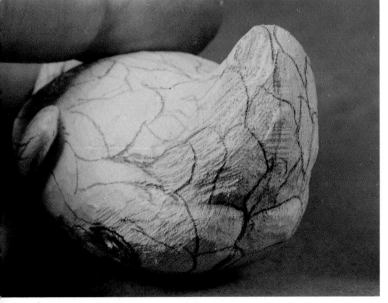

Figure 143. On the lower tail coverts, the contouring clumps are elongated with rounded points.

Figure 144. Use a ruby carver to channel in the contouring lines. On the wings, create a flow with differing elevations on the wood's surface.

Figure 145. With a small pointed ruby carver, use the point to tuck depressions into the contours.

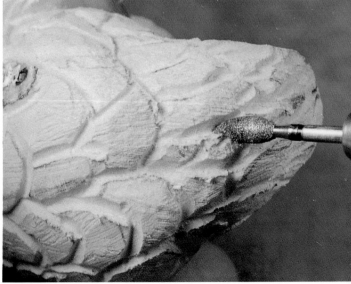

Figure 146. Having some of channels deeper than others will ensure a naturalistic look to the downy clumps.

Figure 147. Note the different layers of hair-like down on the duckling's back.

Figure 148. Using the sharp corner of square-edged stone, texture the winglets and body down. Use the stone to eliminate the sharp corners of the contouring channels.

Figure 149. Curve each stoning stroke.

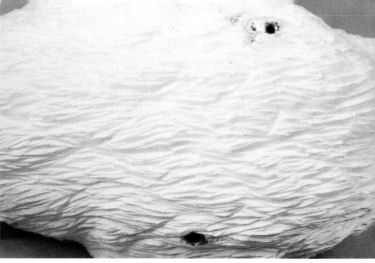

Figure 150. The different levels of the contouring are enhanced with the texturing.

Figure 151. Clean the stoning with the laboratory bristle brush on a mandrel at low speed.

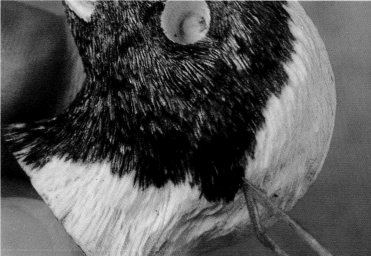

Figure 152. Begin the burning process at the base of the bill and work back towards the back of the head and neck. Do not burn over the pencil marks that match the ones on the body yet.

Figure 153. Clean all burned areas with the toothbrush.

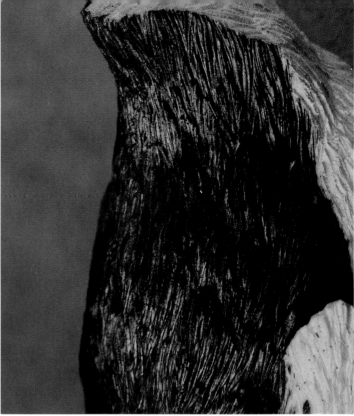

Figure 154. When the head and neck are burned, glue the head to the body matching the pencil marks.

Figure 156. Begin burning the downy clumps at the neck joint and proceed back towards the tip of the tail. The strokes get longer on the back and tail. Curving each stroke gives a realistic appearance to the down. By burning from front to back, each stroke will determine the end of the previous one. Let the beginning of each stroke sink a little deeper and gradually pull up and out at the end of the stroke. This indent burning will enhance the layered look of the hair-like down.

Figure 157. On the duckling's underside, start at the neck joint and proceed back toward the tip of the tail.

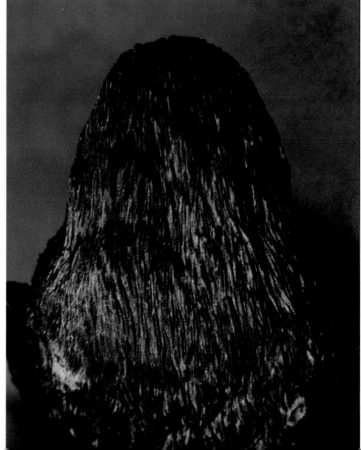

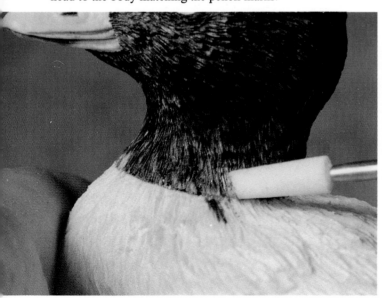

Figure 155. When the glue has hardened, stone along the neck/body joint to vary the contours.

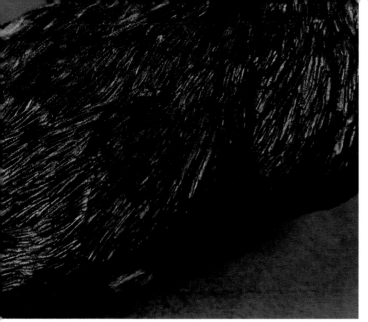

Figure 158. Burn in the texturing on the winglets, starting at the edge of the scapular/upper winglet fluff and proceed toward the tip, flowing the down toward the outer edges. Burn in the texturing on the winglet's underside. Clean the body burning with the toothbrush.

Figure 159. Fill the eye holes with the oily clay, cut the eyes off the wire, and press them into the clay.

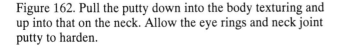

Figure 162. Pull the putty down into the body texturing and up into that on the neck. Allow the eye rings and neck joint putty to harden.

Figure 160. Unlike many other birds, there are slight corners to the front and back of the duckling's eyes. Continue setting the eyes according to the directions in the Bluebird Chapter, and creating the modified points at the eye corners.

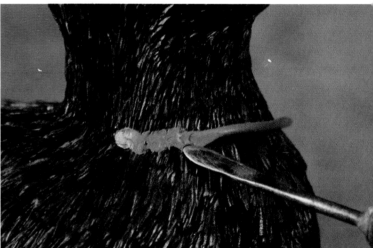

Figure 161. To patch the neck joint, mix a small amount of the epoxy putty. Roll an small worm and press it into the joint all the way around the neck. Plunging the end of the tool in oily clay will prevent the putty from sticking to it.

Figure 163. To prepare the base, cut a piece of 1/4" plywood slightly narrower than a base. Shorten two fat-headed aluminum nails to about one-half inch long. Drill holes slightly larger than the diameter of the nails through the plywood and into the base, but do not go all the way through the bottom. Put the nails in the holes, and put 5 minute epoxy glue over and around the heads. When the glue is dry, remove the plywood from the base.

Figure 165. For stability, flatten one end of a short piece of copper wire, bending it to a right angle, and glue to the flat portion of the bent foot.

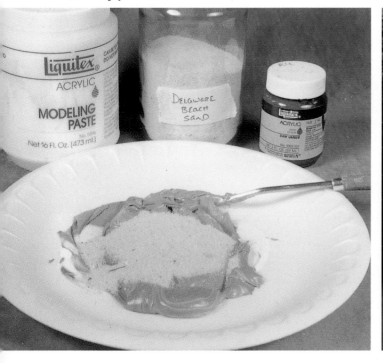

Figure 164. Color some modeling paste with raw umber paint. After the paste and paint are thoroughly mixed, add some sand and mix thoroughly again. Frost this mixture on the plywood base. Dry the modeling paste several minutes with a hair dryer. The outer surface will get hard but it can be broken up and sculpted. Dry it several times and work the surface in between drying until it has an irregular contour. Allow the base to partially dry at least 5 or 6 hours before putting the bird in place.

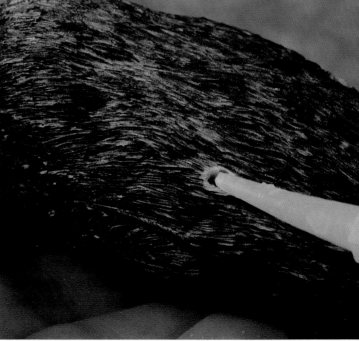

Figure 166. Glue the feet into the body, checking their position carefully and quickly.

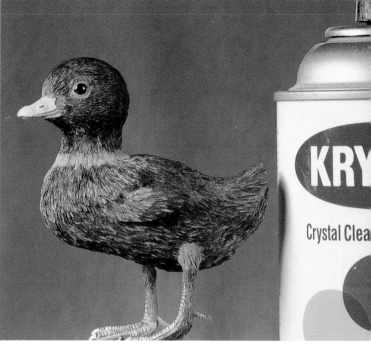

Figure 169. Spray the entire bird with Krylon Crystal Clear 1301.

Figure 167. The bent foot should be positioned inward before the glue dries; the flat foot should slightly toe-in. With the modeling paste and sand mixture not completely dry or hardened all the way through, put the bird in place on the base, pressing the bottom foot wires into the mixture. If the mixture is partially dried, the holes should stay open when you pull the bird out. If the putty has not hardened enough, wait awhile and put the bird in place again.

Figure 170. Apply several coats of gesso dry-brushed with a stiff bristle brush to the entire bird, feet included. When this is dry, carefully scrape the eyes.

Figure 168. To hide the leg attachment joints, mix up a small amount of the epoxy putty. Apply the putty around the joint, and press in the hair-like texturing. Pull the putty into the texturing on the belly. Allow the putty to harden.

# PAINTING THE WOODIE DUCKLING

Liquitex Acrylics (jar) colors:
White = W
Black = B
Payne's grey = PG
Burnt umber = BU
Raw umber = RU
Raw sienna = RS
Yellow oxide = YO

* Indicates that a small amount should be added.

Figure 1. The profile view of the duckling's head.

Figure 2. The top of the bill and head.

Figure 3. There is a light area on the flank just in front of the
tail on each side.

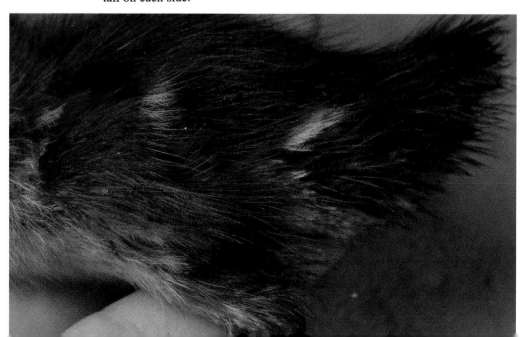

Figure 4. The trailing edge of the upper part of each winglet and scapular fluff has light edges.

Figure 5. The top view of the little winglet.

Figure 6. The underside of the winglet has a light colored center.

Figure 7. The underside of the body.

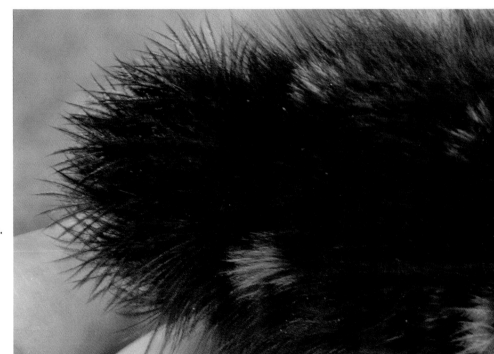

Figure 8. The topview of the tail and rump.

Figure 9. The underside of the tail.

Figure 10. Blending burnt umber and a small amount of payne's grey to a dark brown, apply several basecoats to the top of the head, middle of the hindneck, the stripe behind the eye, eye rings, back, wings, flanks, and the top and underside of the tail.

Figure 12. When you paint the flanks, coat the outer edges of the leg tufts as well. Keeping the edges irregular will ease the blending of the adjacent light color.

Fig. 10

BU + *PG

Figure 13. On the underside of the tail, drag some of the dark mixture irregularly down into the lower tail coverts.

Figure 11. Lightly dry-brush a little of the dark mixture on the ear coverts.

Figure 14. Apply a very watery black wash to all of the dark areas.

Fig. 14

B Wash

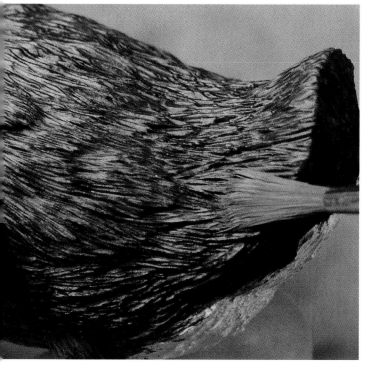

Figure 16. On the head and hindneck, the dry-brushed strokes should be shorter than on the body.

Figure 15. Blending burnt umber, raw sienna, and white, lightly dry-brush highlights onto all of the dark areas. Load the brush with paint, dry most of the paint on a paper towel, and then touch the edges on the surface, dragging them a short distance and pulling off.

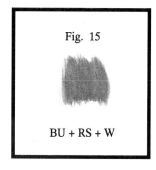

Fig. 15

BU + RS + W

**Woodie Duckling 197**

Figure 17. Apply a thin raw umber wash over all of the highlighted dark areas.

Fig. 17

RU Wash

Figure 18. Apply the highlights and wash several times. Alternate raw umber and burnt umber washes: such as, highlights, RU wash, highlights, BU wash, etc. Keeping the highlights randomly placed will enhance the realistic look to the downy clumps.

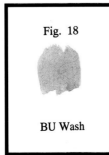

Fig. 18

BU Wash

Figure 19. To make the recessed areas appear even deeper, apply a thin black and burnt umber coat to them.

Figure 20. Blending white, raw umber, and yellow oxide to a light tan, paint in the light spots on the scapular/upper winglet edges and at the base of the tail on each flank. Keep the edges of each light spot feathery and irregular.

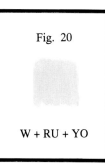

Fig. 20

W + RU + YO

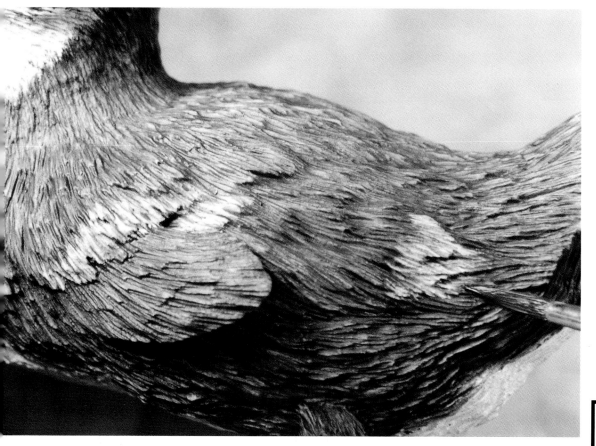

Figure 21. Work a little burnt umber and small amount of payne's grey mixture into the light spot edges. When this is dry, make a wash out of the dark color and wash the lights spots. Highlight the light areas with the light tan color several times, and wash in between with the dark washes.

Fig. 21

BU + *PG

**Woodie Duckling 199**

Figure 22. For the basecoats on the lower tail coverts, belly, insides of the leg tufts, breast, throat, chin, and sides of the head, blend white, yellow oxide, and a small amount of raw umber to a pale yellow.

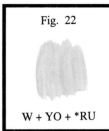

Fig. 22

W + YO + *RU

Figure 23. Drag the pale yellow color into the irregular dark edges on the flanks, chest, neck, and head.

Figure 24. Lightly dry-brush the pale yellow mixture on the lower tail coverts.

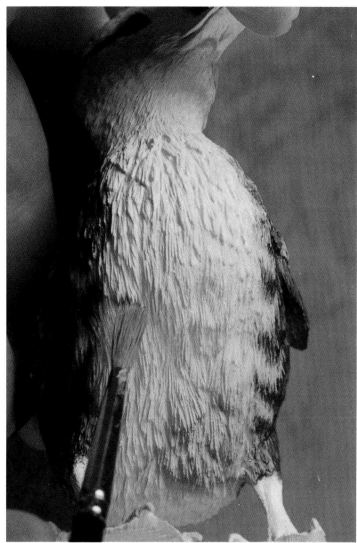

Figure 25. Using straight white and a dry-brush technique, highlight the ends of the downy clumps in all the pale yellow areas.

Figure 26. Blend the dark color basecoat (BU+*PG) and pull into the edges to get a soft, blended transition area.

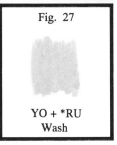

YO + *RU
Wash

Figure 27. Make a wash with yellow oxide and a small amount of raw umber. Load the paint brush, touch to a paper towel to remove some moisture, and then apply to random areas on the underside and sides of the head. Also, dry-brush some of the yellow color on the light spots on each flank at the base of the tail and the light spots on the scapular/upper winglet edges.

Figure 28. Apply a super-thin raw umber wash to all of the light areas on the entire bird.

Figure 29. Blend the light color (W+YO+*RU) and the dark color (BU+*PG) on the ear coverts.

Figure 30. Use the light color to slightly fade out the back of the dark eye stripe. Apply a very thin raw umber wash to the sides of the head.

Figure 31. Blending burnt umber and a small amount of payne's grey to a dark brown, apply several basecoats to all sides of the legs, feet, and toes.

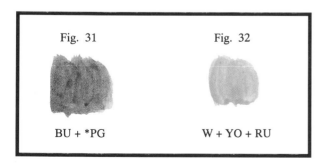

Fig. 31

Fig. 32

BU + *PG

W + YO + RU

Figure 32. For the light areas on the webs, mix white, yellow oxide, and raw umber to a yellowish tan. Apply several coats to the flanges on the side of each toe keeping the edges wavy.

Figure 33. Blend the light and dark colors together several times to get a gradual blend from one to the other.

Figure 34. Mix matte medium into the dark color, and with a fine liner brush, make cross-hatch lines over the light areas.

Figure 35. When this is dry, mix a small amount of gloss medium in a large puddle of water, and apply to the legs, feet, and toes. When dry, paint the claws with undiluted gloss medium.

Figure 36. Blend white, burnt sienna, raw sienna, and a small amount of burnt umber to a dark flesh color, and apply several coats to the sides of both mandibles, the tip of the upper mandible, and the entire underside of the lower mandible.

Figure 38. Add white to the flesh color, and with a liner brush, pull a fine line down the bottom edge of the upper mandible and lower mandible. Apply a wash with a mixture of raw sienna and burnt umber to the entire bill, dry, and then, do the tip a second time.

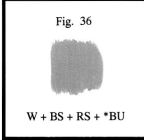

Fig. 36

W + BS + RS + *BU

Fig. 37

BU + PG

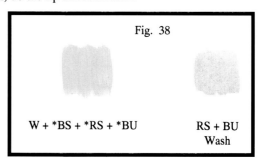

Fig. 38

W + *BS + *RS + *BU

RS + BU
Wash

Figure 37. For the base of the upper mandible, apply several coats of a mixture burnt umber and payne's grey. Work the light and dark colors back and forth until there is a soft blend.

Figure 39. When this is dry, apply an equal mixture of matte and gloss mediums to the bill. Scrape the eyes carefully, and glue the little duckling to its mount.

**Woodie Duckling 205**

Figure 40. The complete woodie duckling!